MW00527078

1. Ordained to Preach

ORDAINED TO PREACH

BOOKS BY CHARLES E. MILLER, C.M.

*To Sow the Seed**
*A Sense of Celebration**
Making Holy the Day
*Communicating Christ***
*Repentance and Renewal****
*Announcing the Good News***
*Breaking the Bread***
*Until He Comes *****
Living in Christ
Love in the Language of Penance
Opening the Treasures
*The Word Made Flesh***
As Rain That Falls
Mother and Disciple

   * with Oscar J. Miller, C.M.
  ** with Oscar J. Miller, C.M. and Michael M. Roebert
*** with John A. Grindel, C.M.

All titles, with the exception of the first three, have been published by Alba House.

ORDAINED
to PREACH
A Theology and Practice
of Preaching

Charles E. Miller, C.M.

"God has given me the grace to be a minister of Christ Jesus... with the priestly duty of preaching the gospel of God." (Rm 15:15)

"By your gift I will proclaim your praise in the great assembly." (Ps 22:26)

ALBA · HOUSE house NEW · YORK

SOCIETY OF ST. PAUL, 2187 VICTORY BLVD., STATEN ISLAND, NY 10314

Library of Congress Cataloging-in-Publication Data

Miller, Charles Edward, 1929-
    Ordained to preach : a theology and practice of preaching /
Charles E. Miller.
        p.   cm.
    Includes bibliographical references.
    ISBN 0-8189-0637-5
    1. Preaching.   I. Title.
BV4211.2.M494   1992
251-dc20   92-16295
                                            CIP

Nihil Obstat:
Msgr. Joseph Pollard, S.T.D.
Censor Deputatus

Imprimi Potest:
Jerome R. Herff, C.M.
Provincial, Province of the West

Imprimatur:
Roger Cardinal Mahony
Archbishop of Los Angeles
August 10, 1991

The *Nihil Obstat* and *Imprimatur* are official declarations
that a book or pamphlet is free of doctrinal or moral
error. No implication is contained therein that those
who have granted the *Nihil Obstat* and Imprimatur agree
with the contents, opinions or statements expressed.

Produced and designed in the United States of America by the
Fathers and Brothers of the Society of St. Paul,
2187 Victory Boulevard, Staten Island, New York 10314,
as part of their communications apostolate.

Printing Information:

Current Printing - first digit	1	2	3	4	5	6	7	8	9	10

Year of Current Printing - first year shown

1992	1993	1994	1995	1996	1997

CONTENTS

Part III: Preparation and Delivery

INTRODUCTION

It is impossible to produce a book on preaching that will produce a preacher. A course in homiletics will not generate the homilist. But the homilist, no matter how naturally talented, will not realize his potential without some good coaching. What is said here of the homilist is paralleled in each art and craft.

And so a book such as this one is of significant value to the homilist and the would-be homilist. It is written by Father Charles E. Miller, C.M. It is the product of the ideal coach — a priest who has taught homiletics to generations of priests while spending the same years as a gifted homilist himself Sunday after Sunday to parish congregations and audiences.

Father Miller's book is rich in motivation, theology, technique, illustration, method and story. Even more so: it is unashamed in its love of the Word of God, in its reverence for that Word, and in its desire that the homilist be captivated (as Isaiah was) by the power and beauty and grace of the Word.

The renewal of the Second Vatican Council is deeply centered on the restoration of the Word of God among us. At the same time, we are called to an awareness of the need for better preaching in our parishes and assemblies.

We are confident that this book will be of great pastoral assistance to all who are charged with the service and ministry of the Word — the breaking of this particular bread of Divine Life in the midst of the assembly.

Roger Cardinal Mahony
Archbishop of Los Angeles
Feast of St. Bartholomew
August 24th

FOREWORD

"By your gift I will proclaim your praise in the
vast assembly." (Ps 22:26)

I have gathered material and ideas for this work on homiletics from many sources, including not only books and academic courses but people. After over thirty-five years of teaching I cannot remember precisely who and what all those sources were. I must, however, in the first place acknowledge my brother, Father Oscar Miller, C.M. who had already been teaching homiletics for fifteen years when I began to follow him in this profession in 1956. From him I derived a knowledge of the most important homiletic principles. I appreciate greatly my Vincentian training at St. Vincent's College in Cape Girardeau, Missouri, and at St. Mary's Seminary in Perryville, Missouri, and the broadening experiences of graduate work with talented men and women, professors and students, at St. Louis University and the University of Southern California. I also value the experience of working with, I don't now how many, diligent seminarians who have gone on to be dedicated priests and from whom I learned more than I can determine. I also thank the innumerable people who have graciously listened to my homilies in the parishes of the Archdiocese of Los Angeles.

One book more than any other has helped shape my approach, and that is *Effective Speaking* by Arthur Edward Philipps which was first published in 1908. I have attempted to

"baptize" the sound principles of this classic work and to focus
upon all aspects of preaching the light of the New Testament
with the goal of helping preachers not only to preach what
Jesus preached but to do it the way he did it. I hope that this
book can serve as a text book in seminaries and be of assistance
to those who have already been ordained. If I seem to concentrate on preaching by priests, I do not intend to exclude
deacons or lay people; it is simply that over the years my efforts
and my heart have been dedicated primarily to seminarians
and priests.

For reading the manuscript and for their suggestions and
encouragement, I am grateful to my brother, Father Oscar
Miller, C.M., and to my former students, Father Dennis
Mongrain of the Archdiocese of Los Angeles and Father
Howard Lincoln of the Diocese of San Bernardino, California.

I especially thank God that as a priest "by his gift I have
been privileged to proclaim his praise in the vast assembly."

Biblical Abbreviations

OLD TESTAMENT

Genesis	Gn	Nehemiah	Ne	Baruch	Ba
Exodus	Ex	Tobit	Tb	Ezekiel	Ezk
Leviticus	Lv	Judith	Jdt	Daniel	Dn
Numbers	Nb	Esther	Est	Hosea	Ho
Deuteronomy	Dt	1 Maccabees	1 M	Joel	Jl
Joshua	Jos	2 Maccabees	2 M	Amos	Am
Judges	Jg	Job	Jb	Obadiah	Ob
Ruth	Rt	Psalms	Ps	Jonah	Jon
1 Samuel	1 S	Proverbs	Pr	Micah	Mi
2 Samuel	2 S	Ecclesiastes	Ec	Nahum	Na
1 Kings	1 K	Song of Songs	Sg	Habakkuk	Hab
2 Kings	2 K	Wisdom	Ws	Zephaniah	Zp
1 Chronicles	1 Ch	Sirach	Si	Haggai	Hg
2 Chronicles	2 Ch	Isaiah	Is	Malachi	Ml
Ezra	Ezr	Jeremiah	Jr	Zechariah	Zc
		Lamentations	Lm		

NEW TESTAMENT

Matthew	Mt	Ephesians	Ep	Hebrews	Heb
Mark	Mk	Philippians	Ph	James	Jm
Luke	Lk	Colossians	Col	1 Peter	1 P
John	Jn	1 Thessalonians	1 Th	2 Peter	2 P
Acts	Ac	2 Thessalonians	2 Th	1 John	1 Jn
Romans	Rm	1 Timothy	1 Tm	2 John	2 Jn
1 Corinthians	1 Cor	2 Timothy	2 Tm	3 John	3 Jn
2 Corinthians	2 Cor	Titus	Tt	Jude	Jude
Galatians	Gal	Philemon	Phm	Revelation	Rv

ORDAINED TO PREACH

PART ONE

GENERAL PRINCIPLES

"I am eager to preach the gospel ..."
(Rm 1:15)

"Father, keep before us the wisdom and love you have revealed in your Son. Help us to be like him in word and deed."

Prayer from the Seventh Sunday of Ordinary Time

CHAPTER I

PREACHING IN PERSPECTIVE

*"It is not ourselves we preach but Christ Jesus
as Lord and ourselves as your servant for
Jesus' sake." (2 Cor 4:5)*

Deep in my heart I wanted to call this book "To Preach As Jesus Did." I rejected that title and bowed to the wisdom of Biblical criticism which shows that we do not have the *ipsissima verba* of Jesus in every instance in the gospels, and that the evangelists are redactors and not chroniclers. The Pontifical Biblical Commission in its "Instruction on the Historical Truth of the Gospels," April 21, 1964 states: "...the teachings and the life of Jesus were not simply recounted for the mere purpose of being kept in remembrance, but were 'preached' in such a way as to furnish the Church with the foundation on which to build up faith and morals."

The same Instruction points out that Jesus "ensured that his teachings would be deeply impressed on the minds (of his hearers) and would be easily retained in memory by his disciples." My conviction is that this memory included style as well as the content which the evangelists took as their foundational body of instruction for the formation of the gospels. I believe that what is found in the teaching of the gospels reflects not only the message of Jesus but also his method, not indeed in so many words but surely in spirit and in essence. That is why the gospels are both the source of the message and the model for preaching it. And so throughout this book I will regularly refer to how Jesus preached with the goal of learning "to preach as Jesus did."

Liturgical Preaching

The form of preaching which most Catholics experience regularly is liturgical preaching, but this form does not exhaust the Church's mission to preach. Evangelization and catechesis outside the liturgy, and other forms of proclamation by those who share the common priesthood of Christ through baptism-confirmation, are part of that mission.

Qualified lay people may preach in church, even during the liturgy. They may give teaching and they may give witness. This latter is characterized by being presented in the first person singular. Lay preaching, which is either teaching or witness, is quite appropriate at a rosary, a wake service, or during other forms of devotions. Since a lay person may preside at the Liturgy of the Hours in the absence of an ordained minister, lay preaching may be part of this prayer. During the celebration of Mass it is not appropriate to give teaching or witness following the gospel because people may presume that a liturgical homily is being presented. Such preaching may be done before Mass or during the announcement time following the Prayer after Communion. Teaching and witness should ordinarily not be given at the ambo from which the scriptures are proclaimed but from a second lectern, if the speaker requires one.

Canon 766 states: "The laity may be allowed to preach in a church or oratory if in certain circumstances it is necessary, or in particular cases it would be advantageous, according to the provision of the Episcopal Conference and without prejudice to Canon 767, no. 1." The canon referred to, which should not suffer "prejudice," says: "The most important form of preaching is the homily which is part of the liturgy and it is reserved to a priest or deacon." The Pontifical Commission for the Authentic Interpretation of the Code of Canon Law decreed on May 26, 1987 that the diocesan bishop may not dispense from this regulation which reserves the preaching of a liturgical homily to a deacon or priest (I might add that we must presume that the law does not mean to exclude bishops!). The reason the diocesan bishop may not dispense is that canon 767, no. 1 is a constitutive law. This means that of its very essence the homily is a form of preaching which can be done only by ordained ministers.

Since only the ordained can preach the homily, they should dedicate themselves to this ministry with singular attention. This refers especially to the presiders at Eucharist, bishops and priests. They should leave aside tasks which others can do so that they may prepare well for homiletic preaching which they alone can do. A surgeon who has perfected the intricate techniques of open heart surgery does no favor to his patients when they are deprived of his expertise because he spends his time in duties which his secretary can accomplish better than he. Especially in these days when we are called to collaborative ministry, priests should not allow administrative duties to preoccupy them, not because they are unworthy of priests, but because priests ought to dedicate themselves to their specific duty in the Body of Christ. In the body ears do not attempt to fulfill the function of eyes.

In a very practical way some priests enter into their appointment book the time they set aside to prepare their Sunday homily. They make a point of not allowing some other need to interfere. If someone wants their attention, they reply, in complete honesty, that they already have an appointment, and their appointment is with the hundreds of people who will hear them preach on Sunday. They also do not neglect to determine a time to prepare daily homilies.

This book is concerned almost exclusively with preaching during the liturgy. It treats primarily of the liturgical homily, especially the eucharistic homily. After Vatican II the term "homily" has come to have a restricted sense. It is reserved to that form of preaching which is integral to the celebration of the Sacraments and the Liturgy of the Hours. Within the liturgy preaching is ordinarily the prerogative of the presider. It is a presidential function. Only by exception may a bishop, priest, or deacon other than the celebrant, the presider, give the homily. The summit of this type of preaching is the eucharistic homily. At Mass he who breaks the bread of the Eucharist for the people also breaks open the Word of God for them.

Some priests favor a rotational system whereby priests of the parish take turns preaching at all the Masses on Sunday (an opportunity, some might call it a luxury, which is possible only in those parishes which have more than one priest). Advocates maintain that the rotational system makes for a better prepared homily since the "burden" of preaching a homily every Sunday is lifted. I personally doubt the validity of this argument, but more importantly liturgical norms indicate that only by exception should someone other than the presider preach. It is not correct for the presider routinely to surrender this important function to someone else. Also, since preaching is the primary priestly apostolate, it is not too much to ask a priest to put aside sufficient time each week in order to prepare for this apostolate and to forego other duties in its favor.

Preaching is Prophetic

Preaching by an ordained minister, especially during the celebration of the liturgy, is not merely one among many forms of oral communication; rather, this form of preaching is unique in that it is prophetic, not in the sense that it proclaims the future or that it is a challenge to the people, though it may be such, but in the sense that the core of authentic preaching is not words about God, but the word of God itself. Preaching is an experience in faith for both the preacher and the listener.

A conscientious preacher must allow the truth of God as presented by the Church in scripture and tradition to be like the air he breathes. There should be no time when the Word of God is not part of him, as we will see in the next chapter on Homiletic Spirituality.

Preaching Is Incarnational

Preaching is like Jesus, divine and human. The divine word comes to us clothed in human words. The word of God is communicated through the words of his people. We must not rely on a human approach which is so devoid of a foundation in divine truth that we end up with gimmicks and platitudes and not the word of God. On the other hand the incarnational aspect of preaching must not be ignored. Knowledge of scripture and theology, and even holiness of life, in themselves are not enough. Prayerful study and reflection must be translated into a human expression. The humanness of the word is either a smooth vehicle for conveying God's word or it is a halting, unreliable jalopy which is enveloped in its own polluting and obscuring exhaust. We need to follow the solid principles of speech delivery and sermon composition so that God's truth may be communicated properly to his people. We cannot reject the necessity of using the proper techniques in preaching.

Whatever should be the title of this book, I hope it will help those who are called to preach in the Church not only to proclaim the truth, but to do it as Jesus did.

SUMMARY:

Preaching is prophetic: authentic preaching is not words about God but the word of God itself. Preaching is also incarnational; it is like Jesus, human and divine: the divine word comes to us clothed in human words. The goal of homiletic preaching is not only to preach what Jesus preached but to do it the way he did it.

EXERCISE:

What is your view of the opinion that all a preacher needs is sincerity and truth, that techniques get in the way of the Word? Is it realistic to state that authentic preaching is prophetic? Can we really capture the way Jesus preached? What practical steps need to be taken so that preaching is really primary in the ministry of a priest?

CHAPTER II

HOMILETIC SPIRITUALITY

"God has given me the grace to be a minister of Christ Jesus... with the priestly duty of preaching the gospel." (Rm 15:15)

Almost every article or book on Catholic preaching these days laments its sorry state. I for one am weary of the negativity, and at times the sarcasm, of this approach because I suspect that preaching is not as bad as some would make it out to be, although I am willing to admit that it is not as good as it should be. Critics and perhaps many practitioners do not seem to realize how absorbing and consuming preaching has to become if, by God's grace, it is to be effective. Preaching must be part of a priest's entire life. He must develop a homiletic spirituality.

Full, active participation in the sacred liturgy is the indispensable source of the true Christian spirit, but within that broad spirit there are many specific expressions. God does not call everyone in the Church to follow the same personal spirituality. Part of priestly spirituality is the truth that priests are ordained to be preachers. It is not merely that priests carry out a function, which is to preach, but that the office of preaching is intrinsic to the sacramental character of ordination. Pope St. Gregory the Great wrote in his *Pastoral Guide:* "Anyone who is ordained a priest undertakes the task of preaching.... If a priest does not know how to preach, what kind of cry can such a dumb herald utter? It was to bring this home that the Holy Spirit descended in the form of tongues on the first pastors, for he causes those whom he has filled to speak out."

Priests are sometimes spoken of as "sent to preach," but I find that it is more exact to reflect the truth that Christ draws us to himself as he continues his ministry in the Church as preacher rather than to suggest that Christ stays behind somewhere and sends priests forward in his name. Jesus so sent the first preachers before he offered himself on the cross, but since he has been exalted as both Lord and Christ through his paschal mystery he is now present and active throughout the whole world, especially through the sacraments, including that of ordination. It may be said, then, that priests are "called to preach." This phrase indicates that preaching is a vocation; it is part of the call to be a priest. A priest *is* a preacher. That is an aspect of his identity through ordination. With that last realization I arrived at the title of this book, "Ordained to Preach."

I have interviewed innumerable candidates applying for admission to the seminary. A routine question is, "Why do you want to be a priest?" Usual answers are "I want to serve people," or "I want to be holy," or "I want to love God." I cannot recall ever hearing a candidate say, "Because I want to preach." And yet by ordination priests are called to embrace preaching as part of their lives, as the relationship of parents to their children has become part of their lives. A pastor may assign an associate to be in charge of the religious education program in the parish, and he may take for himself the direction of ministry to the sick, but we are not assigned to the ministry of preaching, nor do we take it for ourselves. Preaching is insepa-rable from priesthood. In fact, Pope Paul VI in his first encyclical, *Ecclesiam Suam,* declared that preaching is the primary apostolate of priests. *The Decree on the Ministry and Life of Priests* by Vatican II added that "Priests as co-workers with their bishop have as their primary duty the proclamation of the gospel of God to all" (no. 4). Priests can apply to themselves the words of the prophet Malachi: "The lips of the priest are to keep knowledge, and instruction is to be sought from his mouth because he is the messenger of the Lord of hosts" (2:7).

Some priests upon hearing this emphasis on preaching wonder about their sacramental ministry. After all the priest is the "sacramental person" of the Catholic community, charged with presiding at the celebration of the sacraments (granting the exception of marriage and ordination), especially the Eucharist. Should we not say that the celebration of the sacraments is the first apostolate of priests?

Three points need to be kept in mind. The first is that one form of preaching precedes the sacraments and leads to their celebration. Preaching outside the liturgy, which includes evangelization and catechesis, is directed to the liturgy as its summit, as is all the activity of the Church (*Constitution on the Liturgy,* no. 10). This type of preaching is an apostolate, the goal of which is "that all who are made children of God by faith and baptism should come together to praise God in the midst of his Church, to take part in her sacrifice, and to eat the Lord's supper" (*Ibid*). In other words, the first apostolate of the priest in a sequence of activities is to lead people to the liturgy through preaching.

The second point is that even within the liturgy, which is the summit of the Church's activity, preaching retains its primary importance. The liturgical renewal has insisted that sacraments should not be celebrated without a proclamation of the Word, which includes preaching. This ideal should be followed, even when the law is not rigorous: for example, a weekday Mass without preaching lacks an important element, and even an individual celebration of penance is incomplete without scripture and a word from the priest. Scripture and sacraments go together, and scripture within the liturgy is not to be separated from preaching.

The third point is that in the traditional sense preaching is a sacrament. Limiting the concept to those seven actions of the Church which Trent defined as the sacraments represents a development in theology which depended on a narrow use of the term. Vatican II returned us to its traditional and broader meaning by indicating that "the Church is a sacrament or sign of intimate union with God and of the unity of the human race" (*Lumen Gentium,* no. 1). Liturgical preaching fits this notion of a sacrament and can be included even in the catechism definition of a sacrament as "an outward sign instituted by Christ to give grace." The priest, the sacramental person in the Church, is a preacher. Preaching must be, therefore, a consideration in his approach to his spirituality.

Preaching Oneself

Priests have often heard the warning that they must not preach themselves. In a human sense this caution is necessary. The pulpit is not a place to show off nor it is a means for drawing attention to the preacher. In a theological sense, however , the caution is off the mark. The effective preacher is an embodiment of the Word of God, Christ himself. The Word is part of his being by ordination and should also be such by study, reflection, and holiness. A priest is called to proclaim Christ from the depths of his priestly identity as preacher of the Word. Jacques Bossuet, the seventeenth century French Bishop and renowned preacher said, "One speaks from the pulpit, but preaching takes place in the heart."

People know when a preacher does not speak from within, from his heart. They can tell when he has drawn his ideas from books, even those of the Bible, without having assimilated them through prayer and reflection. They recognize the difference between preaching oneself and preaching Christ who is part of oneself. A parishioner complained to a priest that he caused only dismay because he did not practice what he preached. The priest replied, "What you say may be true, but there would be even more dismay if I were to preach what I practice." Whatever may have been the facts in that situation, we can be sure that people are moved when human words communicate the Divine Word. St. Albert the Great, the mentor of St. Thomas Aquinas, wrote: "A sermon which proceeds from a preacher's innermost being warms and gladdens the heart like wine and is often brought back to mind and pondered."

Homiletic Spirituality

Homiletic spirituality means that a priest sees preaching as his call from God to which he must respond with diligent study and devout prayer. He does not separate preaching from his spiritual life any more than he would dismiss his need to express sorrow for sins or to offer thanksgiving for blessings.

Some authors would reprimand priests for always asking the question, "How can I preach this to the people?" They would have priests read scripture and study theology for its intrinsic merit or for the benefit which priests can derive for themselves personally. They fear that priests may refuse to face challenges to themselves by always turning teachings into applications for the people. That danger must be admitted, but it is not a pitfall for priests who have an authentic homiletic spirituality which requires that in every instance they make truth part of their being and not merely a list of data stored in their mind's computer.

While needing to take care of himself spiritually, a priest must see that there is no sound concern for himself unless it focuses on his true identity, and that identity is to be a priest who is a preacher. The Code of Canon Law indicates that for priests to pursue holiness they are "first of all faithfully and untiringly to fulfill the duties of pastoral ministry" (Canon 276). First among these duties of ministry is that of preaching.

Research studies conclude that priests are happy and spiritually sound when their ministry is not only "reactional" but "intentional." We must react to the needs of our people when and where they arise. This reaction has been called the ministry of the doorbell and the telephone. Someone expressed a truism when he said, "I was upset with all the interruptions in my ministry until I realized that interruptions are my ministry." And yet every priest needs a task to which he creatively and deliberately applies himself. Such is "intentional" ministry. For every priest preaching should be an intentional ministry as well as a means to holiness.

Nourishment for God's People

Holiness embraces a relationship with the Holy Spirit. The Holy Spirit conceived Christ in the womb of Mary and that event completely changed her life. The Holy Spirit has the power to conceive Christ anew within the words of authentic preachers in the Church, a reality which should influence every moment of a priest's life. A priest is like a woman who is pregnant or who is nursing a child at her breast. Such a woman takes nourishment for her own health and well being, but if she understands what it means to be a mother she thinks about everything she eats and drinks and judges how it will affect her child. She simply cannot eat or drink for herself alone without any consideration for the welfare of her child. A priest who is true to his calling never reads or studies or thinks or has any experience for himself alone. He knows that his words are to be nourishment for his people. He always has in mind the good of his people who call him "Father," a title which, as it applies both to the priest and to God himself, includes what we consider to be maternal as well as what we consider to be paternal qualities.

St. Albert wrote: "Preachers have the gospel in their heart through love and understanding, on their lips through their preaching, and in their hands through the accomplishment of their work." And so I say, always — in every instance — without any exception — a priest should ask himself the preacher's question, "What is the homily in this experience?" This question should be asked regarding not only the study of scripture and theology but other reading, watching TV, going to movies, and sharing in any human experience. When does a priest prepare his homily? A priest who embraces homiletic spirituality is always preparing his homily because there is a homily in everything. The preacher must learn to see God not only in Jesus Christ but in the members of his body, not only in the saints and sinners of the past but in the saints and sinners of the present. The preacher through reflection sees divine reality not only in the actions of salvation history recorded in the Bible but also in God's actions in our world today.

We do not live in two worlds, one religious and one secular. We live in God's world. God is indeed everywhere, and in his creation he is revealed as the artist is seen in his art. God works according to consistent themes so that what we know of him through the visible leads us by his grace to the invisible. We are in contact with the material and we touch the spiritual. There is a transcendent meaning to human experience. A preacher must be a contemplative, not only of the Creator but of his creatures. The image of a contemplative which some people have is that of a person who goes off by himself to a remote and quiet place where he attempts to detach himself completely from his surroundings, and blots out everything from his mind in order to allow the Lord to manifest himself. I call this "closed-eyed" spirituality. This form of contemplation is not sufficient for a preacher. A preacher must also have "open-eyed" spirituality.

The international Synod of Bishops at Rome in 1971 wrote in the document, *De Sacerdotio Ministeriali:* "Priests should give themselves to the contemplation of the Word of God and daily take the opportunity to examine the events of life in the light of the gospel so that, as faithful and attentive hearers of the Word, they may become true ministers of the Word."

The Perfect Preacher

The gospels present Jesus to us as the ideal preacher who lives with eyes open to the meaning of creation and human life. Jesus was perceptive. He asked himself the homiletic questions: "What does the reign of God resemble? To what shall I liken it?" (Lk 13:18). He saw an example of divine guidance in shepherds. He experienced zeal in fishermen. He derived a lesson from the tragic death of the people upon whom the tower fell at Siloam. He perceived aspects of the kingdom in the pearl of great price, in the net full of good and bad fish, and in the growth of a mustard seed. He loved wedding parties because they mirror the joyful union of God with his people. He accepted invitations to dinner because food and drink and fellowship are a reflection of the meaning of the eucharistic celebration.

When Jesus spent whole nights in prayer, he did not speak with his Father the whole time. In the presence of his Father and guided by the Holy Spirit, he reflected on the events of that day. He thought of the people whose needs he had met and whose stories continued to echo in his mind. He could wrap the message he preached in wonderful parables, metaphors, and analogies because he was always reflecting on the significance of human experience.

One delightful result of following the example of Jesus, of always looking for sermon material, is that we are constantly praying. We are enlightened by God's truth and warmed by his love. We begin to appreciate the wonder and beauty to be found through living in God's world. God is always near us, not only within us by the divine indwelling, but around us in people and in events. We become aware of the divine presence, not only during the celebration of liturgies, but also as we share human sorrow and human joy. We discover spiritual realities in seeing a movie, in watching a ball game, in going to dinner, in playing sports, in enjoying friends, and in finding the rest of sleep. A priest does not have to retreat in order to be a prayerful person. In fact, he is called, not to walk away from the world and human experience, but to enter into them.

St. Hilary, Bishop and Doctor of the Church, reflected homiletic spirituality in this prayer which he offered during a sermon on the Trinity: "I am well aware, almighty God and Father, that in my life I owe you a most particular duty. It is to make my every thought and word speak of you. In fact, you have conferred on me this gift of speech, and it can yield no greater return than to be at your service. It is for making you known as Father, the Father of the only begotten God, and preaching this to the world."

I know of only one way to be holy, and that is to follow the plan of God the Father that we are to become conformed to the image of his Son (Rm 8:29). One aspect of that plan for priests is homiletic spirituality which leads us to become a preacher like Jesus Christ.

SUMMARY:

The preacher is like a woman who is pregnant or who is nursing her child at the breast who can no longer think only of herself but must always keep her child in mind. A priest is a preacher by ordination, and when he is true to his calling he never reads or studies or has any experience for himself alone; he must always be thinking about nourishing his people through his preaching.

Exercise:

What are some practical implications of asserting that a priest is a preacher by ordination? Express your understanding of what homiletic spirituality means. Think of some recent experience or movie or TV shows. Answer the question, "What is the homily in this?"

CHAPTER III

THE PRAYER OF A HOMILIST

*"First of all I ask that supplications, prayers,
petitions, and thanksgiving be offered for
everyone.... This is good and pleasing
to God our Savior." (1 Tm 2:1)*

From the time I entered the high school seminary in 1943 I can remember hearing that a priest must be a man of prayer. Since a priest is by necessity also a homilist, it follows that a homilist must be a man of prayer.

Without prayer we cut ourselves off from God's grace. It is like pulling the plug on an appliance. Without electricity it simply does not work. A priest who consistently does not pray rejects his calling as an instrument of God. Of course in the matter of the sacraments the people are safeguarded because of our doctrine of "ex opere operato," but I know of no teaching of the Church which applies that doctrine to preaching. Unfortunately for the people, preaching does not bring about its effect "ex opere operato." I think that a priest without prayer puts God in the position of acting directly without the help of his chosen instrument. A priest cannot expect to preach authentically so that his homily is not words about God but the word of God itself if he is not actively in union with God through prayer. St. Isidore said, "Learning unsupported by grace may get into your ears, but it will never reach the heart,"

and preaching which is not from the heart through prayer is
not effective. The prayer of the preacher must be one of loving
union with God as well as of petition for help and guidance in
preaching.

The Liturgy of the Hours

There is a form of prayer which is particularly appropriate, even necessary, for a preacher to accomplish his mission,
and that is apostolic prayer. Apostolic prayer is one of union
not only with God but with his people. It is Church prayer. The
preeminent form of apostolic prayer is the breviary, the divine
office, which today is properly called the Liturgy of the Hours.
It is vital to effective preaching. I am not bold enough to say
that preaching has fallen off in proportion to our letting the
office go, but I do believe that preaching is brought to fruition
through a faithful and complete praying of the Liturgy of the
Hours.

The doctrine of the Church is that "full, active participation in the sacred liturgy is the primary and indispensable
source of the true Christian spirit" (*Constitution on the Liturgy*,
no. 14). An important component of the liturgy is the divine
office. Every priest needs some personal, private devotions to
suit his individual needs. Saying the rosary, making the sta-
tions, spending time before the Blessed Sacrament are examples of time-tested devotions in the Church, but they must
not replace the Liturgy of the Hours, especially for priests.
Priests promise to pray the entire Liturgy of the Hours, and
they are so required by law (canon 1174). Although morning
prayer and evening prayer are the cardinal hours and should
not be omitted without a serious reason, the other hours are
also important, even though a less serious reason is needed to
omit them. The truth is that a priest who consistently skips the
Liturgy of the Hours deprives the people of the Church of the
value of this prayer to which they are entitled and he places his

preaching on a foundation of sand rather than on solid rock.

Priests who have been around a while have seen a lot of changes in the office over the past generation: abbreviations, revisions, translations, rearrangements, and even a new name for the book. But through all the developments in our time and during past ages, one ingredient remains constant: the psalms are the heart of the Church's prayer book. Since they are inspired by the Holy Spirit, they are the right way to pray. They are a gift which should not be ignored, especially by a preacher.

Apostolic Praying: In the Person of Others

Because the psalms are part of the official, public prayer of the Church, they are offered in the name of the Church and for the Church. "Church" means people — real, live people, not some abstraction. As we go through the psalms we find almost every possible human emotion, need, and sentiment. We will not be able to identify with these feelings in every instance, but they do reflect the conditions and states of mind of those to whom we preach. To foster an understanding of how to pray the psalms, my confrere, Father Philip Van Linden, C.M., and I, when we were giving workshops on the Liturgy of the Hours in the 1970's, coined the term, "apostolic praying." Apostolic praying means offering the psalms not only for people but *in their very person*. It must be clear that apostolic praying involves entering into the lives of our people. It means becoming the heart and the voice of others. It is the prayerful corollary of the rhetorical principle of Reference to Experience which will be treated in Chapter VI.

Preparation for this prayer as well as for preaching involves reading the newspaper, watching the news on TV, and above all observing closely and listening carefully to our people. To know people is to know both how to preach and how to pray. Consider Psalm 88 which is part of Night Prayer on Friday. It is offered at a time when a lot of people, having left work thinking "TGIF," are relaxing in the company of family or friends at a nice dinner or at a show with pleasant expectations for the weekend. There is nothing like that for the person of Psalm 88. We say of a person in trouble that he is behind the eight ball. This persons is behind two eight balls. He complains to God:

> "You have taken away my friends
> and made me hateful in their sight.
> Friend and neighbor you have taken away:
> my one companion is darkness."

In my entire life I have never felt at any time that my one companion was darkness. I can hardly think of a more bleak outlook, and yet it is a reality for some people, not only for the hungry and the homeless but for the abused wife, the abandoned husband, the unloved child. We join with these people in their own prayer or we make up what is lacking in those who do not pray. United with desolate people and in their person we offer Psalm 88 to God and say:

> "I call to you, Lord, all the day long;
> To you I stretch out my hands.
> Lord, why do you reject me?
> Why do you hide your face?"

Psalm 71 is the prayer of someone who is about seventy-one years of age, maybe a little older, who calls out to the Lord:

> "Do not reject me now that I am old;
> when my strength fails do not forsake me.
> Now that I am old and grey-headed
> Do not forsake me, God."

I can picture elderly men and women almost forgotten in a rest home, enveloped in a weariness which precludes much inclination to pray, or a senility which seems to make praying impossible. When I turn to Psalm 71 during Daytime Prayer on

Monday of Week III, I pray in the person of elderly people. (There was a time when I was young with black hair and I did not know how to say this prayer; then I learned to pray in the person of the elderly but I did not as yet apply this psalm to myself; now without even having to look into the mirror I realize that I must include myself in this prayer.)

Open your breviary to the Office of Readings for Friday of Week II and try offering Psalm 38 in the person of those who have AIDS:

> "My friends avoid me like a leper;
> those closest to me stand afar off.
> I am like the deaf who cannot hear,
> like the dumb unable to speak.
> I count on you, O Lord;
> It is you, Lord God, who will answer."

A religious once told me that Psalm 27 is among her favorites (it is used at Wednesday Evening Prayer of Week I):

> "The Lord is my light and my help;
> whom shall I fear?"

I try to pray in the person of all religious when I say in this psalm:

> "O Lord, hear my voice when I call;
> have mercy and answer.
> It is your face, O Lord, that I seek;
> hide not your face ."

But I also identify with those who have neither a blood family nor a religious family who cry out in the same psalm,

> "Do not abandon or forsake me,
> O God my help!
> Though father and mother forsake me,
> the Lord will receive me."

Of course not all the psalms are in the literary genre of

lament or complaint. We should be in union with the joyful,
trusting people who cry out to God:

> "My happiness lies in you alone.
> He has put into my heart a marvelous love
> for the faithful ones who dwell in his land.
> You will show me the path of life,
> the fullness of joy in your presence,
> at your right hand happiness forever"
> (Psalm 16 at Thursday Night Prayer)

It is a happy experience to offer Psalm 45 in the person
of those who are just celebrating the sacrament of marriage
(Monday Evening Prayer of Week II), and to offer Psalm 103
together with those who have experienced God's mercy in the
sacrament of penance (Wednesday Office of Readings of
Week IV).

The Prayer of Christ

During Daytime Prayer of the first week I come across
Psalm 17. It is troublesome, not because it is negative, but
because it is so positive that I am embarrassed to stand before
God and say:

> "Lord, hear a cause that is just, pay heed to my cry.
> You test me and you find in me no wrong.
> My words are not sinful as are men's words."

Pretty bold! The psalm is apparently the prayer of a man
who has been unjustly accused and who is pleading his inno-
cence in that particular instance, and yet there is a person who
can offer this prayer without qualification in every instance.
That person is Jesus. This psalm reminds me that Jesus prayed
all the psalms. He did so not only in those few instances which
are recorded in the gospels but with the regularity of a good
Jew according to his upbringing in the home of Nazareth. He
was faithful in going to the synagogue and to the temple at the

prescribed times where the psalms formed an integral part of the worship. And Jesus continues to offer these prayers to his heavenly Father in the people of his Mystical Body, the Church. We become his voice and his heart, and because we form one body and one spirit with him, apostolic praying of the psalms is a reality. We can pray in the person of others because Christ is our bond of unity.

It is unthinkable that a preacher in the Catholic Church should be without a lectionary, and it should be equally unthinkable that he should be without a breviary. Preaching is incomplete without prayer, especially the apostolic prayer of the Liturgy of the Hours. This prayer is an integral part of homiletic spirituality. Priests are called not only to preach to people but to be united with them in the daily prayer of the Church.

SUMMARY:

A priest must pray the psalms, not only for his people, but in the person of those whose sentiments are expressed in the psalms. This is apostolic praying.

EXERCISE:

Select several psalms and try praying them in an Apostolic manner. Be specific about persons and their situations which you find reflected in these psalms. Talk about your own experiences with such people.

[For more on the Liturgy of the Hours I refer the reader to my brief treatise, *Making Holy the Day, A Commentary on the Liturgy of the Hours,* which is published by Catholic Book Publishing Co., New York.]

"The mind is a wonderful thing. It starts working the minute you are born, and never stops until you get up to speak in public."

Marti Beckman

CHAPTER IV

PRINCIPLES OF COMMUNICATION

"The one who speaks is to deliver God's message." (1 P 2:11)

Human communication is an extremely difficult art. You may find the words to express your message, but you have no guarantee that your audience will derive from those words the meaning you have in mind. The complexity of the situation is found in the five elements which go to make up the experience of communication.

The first element is the speaker or sender, and the second is the audience or receiver. It is impossible to treat of the one without the other. The two cannot be separated. They are linked as are the two commandments of love. The binding force between them is the third element, the message to be communicated. This message is contained within the fourth element, the medium, which is like a bridge that spans the gap separating the sender from the receiver. The fifth element is the meaning which the receiver creates from the message which the sender has placed within the medium.

Fundamental Principles

Reflection upon the experience of communication yields some fundamental principles. The first is that the sender does not communicate meaning; rather, the receiver shapes meaning from the building blocks with which the sender supplies him. Communication is not the transfer of ideas from one person to another as a secretary moves a document from one file to another. The receiver reacts according to his background: what he has been taught and what he has learned, what he has studied and what he has experienced. This fact is expressed in the ancient Latin axiom: *Quidquid recipitur per modum recipientis recipitur.*

A person on a Southern California freeway sees a bumper sticker which says, "Think Blue." Because he is a sports fan, he immediately thinks of the Los Angeles Dodgers baseball team, since their color is blue, and he happily realizes that a new season is only a few months away. Another person sees the same bumper sticker and concludes that the driver of the car must be a member of the Blue Army and wishes to foster devotion to our Blessed Mother, especially since the driver has a rosary dangling from the rear view mirror. A third person wonders why the driver is advocating a melancholy spirit on a beautiful Southern California day in January when much of the nation is shoveling snow and slipping on ice. From the same message each person has created a distinct meaning.

Meaning includes all that is represented by such words as significance and value, and includes a reaction from the receiver. A person who does not appreciate baseball (poor soul) may understand the "Think Blue" bumper sticker as referring to the Dodgers and not give it a second thought. A baseball fan may love the Dodgers and think happy thoughts, and not blue ones, whereas another baseball fan may hate the Dodgers (poor soul) and feel annoyed about their winning ways.

Meaning can be compared to the way in which people digest food. A number of people can dine on the same food but each one reacts in a distinctive manner. What agrees with one person may upset another, and what may be productive of energy for one may turn only into fat for another. We speak of "digesting" an idea. How we digest the idea determines the meaning we derive from it. Jesus reflected this principle when he told the parable of the farmer who went out to sow seed. The productivity of the seed depended on the type of ground which received it, some of it falling on a footpath, some on rocky ground, some among briers, and some on good soil (Lk 8:4-15).

A second principle is that the medium is not the message. But it is likewise true that a message cannot stand alone. It is never naked. It is always clothed in a medium, and it is the medium which determines whether the receivers will create for themselves the meaning which the sender intends. It is only in that sense that the medium can be said to be the message.

A medium is any means which conveys the message. Language is the most common media or means by which we convey ideas. It may be a single word or a paragraph. It may be a metaphor, an analogy, an anecdote, or a parable. Verbal media can be supplemented by non-verbal media, whether visual or auditory. The word "medium" in this context has a broad denotation.

Since the medium can be separated from the message, the sender (speaker) must select his medium by taking into account the nature of the receivers (audience). In the fifteenth chapter of the gospel according to Luke, the Pharisees and the scribes were murmuring because Jesus welcomed those who were considered to be sinners and ate with them. Jesus responded to his critics by presenting his case to all the people who had gathered. His message was that God sees all sinners as precious and goes in search of them. He looked at his audience and selected three media for the same message. He spoke first to the men: "Who among you, if he has a hundred sheep and loses one of them, does not leave the ninety-nine in the wasteland and follow the lost one until he finds it?" Then he spoke to the women: "What woman, if she has ten silver pieces and loses one, does not light a lamp and sweep the house in a diligent search until she has retrieved what she lost?" Then to everyone he told the story which we call the parable of the prodigal son. He gave three presentations: the lost sheep, the lost coin, and the lost sons. He used three media for the same message in order to help his hearers create meaning from their background.

Understanding the Medium

A preacher must first be concerned with determining the message of God's revelation and the Church's teaching since he does not make up his own message. The first step is to study the medium since we cannot arrive at the message which the sender intends if we do not understand his medium.

In Shakespeare's play, *Hamlet,* Polonius in speaking to the Queen states that "Brevity is the soul of wit..." (Act II, Scene 2). Someone who hears this statement today might conclude that Polonius is talking about a sense of humor, since that is what we generally understand by the word "wit," but in Shakespeare's time the word "wit" meant wisdom. Brevity is the mark of a wise person who knows what must be said and what may be left unsaid. We have to understand Shakespeare's medium if we hope to arrive at the message he intended.

Sometimes we hear a person remark, "I never stand on ceremonies." We probably conclude that the person is not given to formality. The quotation is from Shakespeare's play, *Julius Caesar* (Act II, Scene 2). Caesar had been warned by a soothsayer: "Beware the Ides of March." His enemies were planning a coup; they intended to assassinate Caesar at the Senate. Calphurnia, Caesar's wife, was deeply troubled and feared for his life and begged him not to go to the senate. She said, "Caesar, I never stood on ceremonies, yet now they fright me." By ceremonies she meant omens which augured ill for Caesar. By stating that she never stood on ceremonies, she was saying that she was not a superstitious person. Anyone who reads her statement "I never stood on ceremonies" according to the manner in which people use it today misses the point.

A failure to grasp the significance of a medium — in this case, language or the spoken word — in its historical, cultural, and social setting leads a receiver to create a meaning which the sender did not intend. We should not read Shakespeare as if his plays were recently composed for Broadway. That is a form of literary fundamentalism which does not do justice to the great dramatist. Nor can we expect to derive the correct message from the scriptures and other theological sources by reading them the way we read the morning newspaper. Fundamentalism, or literalism, in scripture and theology is a serious affront to the way in which God has chosen to communicate his message to us.

Discovering the Message

Preachers are called to discover the message within scripture and other Church sources, a process sometimes called "invention," from the literal meaning of the Latin, "to come upon." This task involves peeling away the medium in order to get to the message. It uses the approach of contemporary exegetes which considers such things as historical background, cultural expression, and literary genre. Literalists mistake the medium for the message and create a meaning which God did not intend to communicate through the human author.

The first question we must ask is, not what do the words of scripture mean now, but what did they mean at the time of their composition. A simple example of this principle can be drawn from the sixteenth chapter of St. John's gospel. Jesus, recognizing that the apostles were upset because he was about to leave them, said: "When a woman is in labor she is sad that her time has come. When she has borne her child, she no longer remembers her pain for joy that a man has been born into the world." Some people believe that this passage reflects a prejudice against female babies because the translation says that the woman has joy that "a man has been born into the world." Actually the original Greek word which has been translated as "man" does not mean a male but a human being. The revised edition of the New American Bible has improved the translation by using the word "child" in place of "man." The point is that one must understand the medium. In some instances in the New Testament, the distinction between the medium and the message is so clear that readers readily accept it. When Jesus declares in the tenth chapter of St. John's gospel that he is the Good Shepherd, no one concludes that Jesus was a keeper of sheep. To take the word "shepherd" literally is to accept the medium as if it were the message.

Taking the Medium To Be the Message

Mistaking the medium for the message is the error which is common among literalists. Some people want to know how big the whale had to be in order to swallow Jonah without harming him. When they are told that the question is irrelevant they become indignant and ask with more than a hint of accusation, "Don't you believe that God has the power to create such a whale?" But the message is not that God made a great fish which is larger than any we now know of. The author of the Book of Jonah told a parable, as Jesus would do later, in a dramatic and picturesque fashion. Jonah had refused to accept the mission to preach repentance to the people of Nineveh (an ancient city opposite the modern city of Mosul in Iraq). He hated these Gentiles who were traditional enemies of Israel and he wanted God to hurl destruction upon them rather than pour out his mercy upon them. When he tried to steal away from God by ship, he was thrown overboard by the sailors. God commanded a great fish to swallow him and then spew him safely upon the shore. God by this action said to Jonah: "Do you now get the point that I mean business: I want you to preach to the people of Nineveh?" When Jonah complied, the people repented. The Book of Jonah is not concerned with fish but with people. The message is: God wants people, even Gentiles, to repent and he gives them the means to do so. When you receive this message, you are in a position with God's grace to understand more about the meaning of God's mercy. The message of the story is concerned not with how big Jonah's fish was but how big God's heart is.

As some people read the initial chapters of the Book of Genesis, they mistake the medium for the message. They think that Genesis, because it says God created the world in six days, contradicts the hypothesis of evolution, even a theistic one. Others who are worried by scientific findings resort to stipulating that a day in Genesis need not be one of twenty-four hours, that a day could represent an entire geological era. This stipulation is not only absurd (since, for example, there is no sun until the fourth day even though there is vegetation on the third day) but entirely unnecessary. Concordism, the effort to reconcile the Bible with modern science, is naive. The Bible is not a scientific treatise. It is a book of faith which uses media which are appropriate for the people for whom it was first written. It is the message which is intended, and the message is that God is the wise creator of the heavens and the earth. From that message, and not from a description of six days, we can derive the meaning intended by God.

It may be that a century from now someone may find an Easter homily which one of us has written in which we refer to a beautiful sunrise. That person may think that we were pretty uninformed scientifically, because the sun does not rise or set, but remains stable while the earth rotates. In our sermon we have used a perfectly acceptable manner of speaking which has nothing to do with science. Our message in this sermon is that the rising sun is a symbol of the rising of God's Son from the dead, but this reader in the future will never arrive at the meaning intended if he thinks that the medium is the message.

Truth, Fact, and Fiction

The message of God's revelation and the teaching of the Church is truth. Truth may be contained within a medium which is either factual or fictitious. What matters is the message, the truth. We believe in the death and resurrection of Jesus as a fact of faith, and yet we must still penetrate to the truth of this mystery. It is possible for a person to accept the fact of the death and the resurrection of Jesus and still not grasp its message. Those who miss the message cannot derive the meaning. We state a fact in the words of the Creed, "He suffered, died, and was buried; on the third day he rose again." We proclaim the message, the truth and not merely the fact, in the eucharistic acclamation, "Dying you destroyed our death, rising you restored our life." With that message we can begin to understand something about the meaning of the paschal mystery, the truth of the death and resurrection of Jesus.

The Bible is God's revelation of his truth. Revelation is more than information about God; it is an invitation to enter into his covenant of love. Some media in the Bible are factual; others are fictitious. In either case God presents to us his message which he wishes us to absorb in faith so that we may embrace the meaning which he intends. The four evangelists were not chroniclers. They did not record events simply because they happened, but because they contain a message of God's truth. In contrast many people who control our news media are obsessed with determining all the facts in the most minute detail, usually without much appreciation of their significance. They follow the thinking of Joe Friday of the old TV show, "Dragnet," who used to insist with a witness, "Just the facts, ma'am, just the facts." In contrast with that insistence, scripture and preaching are concerned with truth.

Noise Factors and Challenges

Adding to the complexity of communication are noise factors, which preachers must work to eliminate from their presentations. A noise factor is anything which gets in the way of effective communication. It is like static which interferes with radio or television reception. Static is distracting. If it is too strong, it moves people to flip the dial. Noise factors in a sermon are distracting too and may move the audience to turn their attention elsewhere. Some preachers have the habit of using a common noise factor, vocalized pauses. They preach something like this: "In today's gospel Jesus *uh* wants all of us to *uh* realize that we must *uh* take discipleship *uh-uh-uh* seriously." This type of noise factor makes it difficult for the people to take the preacher seriously. If the noise factors become too numerous, many people will simply stop listening. Theological jargon, incorrect grammar, unacceptable pronunciations, improper use of words, muttering rather than enunciating — all are noise factors. Meaningless gestures, poor posture, insufficient eye contact, reading from a manuscript, referring to notes, putting on and taking off eye glasses — all are noise factors.

Many people are sensitive to what is termed non-inclusive language. That is why the word "men" was officially dropped from the consecration during the eucharistic prayer, and we now say, "... will be shed for all." Living languages change. At one time the word "men" referred to human beings, but no longer. To use it in that larger sense is often a noise factor. The translation of John 16:21 as "she no longer remembers her pain for joy that a man has been born into the word," is not only misleading; it is also a noise factor for many people.

A preacher might say in a homily that Jesus had a liberal approach to the law. Although the word "liberal" is a perfectly good word with a very positive meaning, it has been made to have negative political connotations for some people. It is a noise factor. Since the preacher does not intend to talk politics, he would do better to choose another word, such as "broad" or "freeing."

A preacher must make serious efforts to avoid noise factors since they interfere with the message, but he must not be afraid to offer challenges to people even though they do not wish to hear such preaching. The Book of Sirach reminds us: "Refrain not from speaking at the proper time, and hide not away your wisdom, for it is through speech that wisdom becomes known" (4:23-24). The preacher must conscientiously proclaim the message of the scriptures. He must, for example, teach Catholics that they have duties regarding social justice even if people accuse him of dealing in politics. The parable of Lazarus and the rich man proposes a challenge to an economically comfortable community, as does the story of the Canaanite woman to a racially prejudiced one (26th Sunday of the Year C and 20th Sunday of the Year A). *Mater si, Magistra no* is simply not acceptable for a Catholic regarding the social teachings of the Church. A priest, wishing to avoid a challenge, actually dropped from the *Magnificat* the phrase, "the rich he sent away empty," because he was afraid it would offend the wealthy landowners who were "important" members of his parish. That is not what avoiding noise factors means.

The Complexity of Language

Cardinal Augustin Bea, S.J., speaking mainly of the problem of translating from the Biblical languages, said in a talk at Rome on Jan. 13, 1963: "It is difficult to present truth in human language. Language is certainly a magnificent gift of the Creator which enables us to open our souls to others, to exchange with one another spiritual gifts, knowledge, and mutual love, but at the same time how imperfect and changeable it is. And how limited our knowledge of it often is.

Language leads to innumerable misunderstandings, even in the sacred realm of religious faith. While faithfully preserving true doctrine, we can express it in various ways, according to the mentality and the languages of men." These observations of a great biblical scholar reflect the elements of communication.

The Reality of Grace

An important component of communication during preaching is the reality of grace. The Holy Spirit not only moves the preacher who is open to grace but also the hearers, the audience. Although the preacher cannot communicate meaning, the Holy Spirit helps people to create not only a correct meaning but a meaning which they need to absorb, provided of course they are receptive to the grace which the Holy Spirit offers to them in the words of the preacher. Priests must pray for the guidance of the Holy Spirit — that is a given. But so must the people — and that truth is often forgotten or ignored. The complexity of human communication is compounded by the profundity of the message in preaching, and so prayer by both preacher and audience is indispensable.

SUMMARY:

The elements in communication are: 1) the sender, 2) the receiver, 3) the medium, 4) the message, and 5) the meaning. Communication is not the transfer of ideas. It cannot put meaning into people; it can only elicit meaning from them since receivers create their own meaning. The medium is not the message, but no message ever stands "naked." It is always clothed in some medium. The task of the sender, the communicator, is first to penetrate the medium to find the message. Then through knowing his receivers, the audience, he must select the media which will help them to create meaning. The nature of the media determines to a large extent the meaning which the receivers create.

EXERCISE:

Read the gospel for the Twenty-Fifth Sunday of the Year A (Mt 20:1-16). Consider all five elements of communication within this gospel as well as possible noise factors.

CHAPTER V

FINDING THE MEDIUM: THE FORMS OF SUPPORT

"What comparison can I use for this generation? What are they like?" (Lk 7:31)

Good homilies do not just happen. They are the product of prayer, study, reflection, and hard work. Looking at the readings shortly before Mass and deciding "to say a few words on the gospel" will eventuate in an effective homily only by a miracle of God's grace with no thanks to the homilist. Particularly demanding is the finding of an appropriate medium. Such does not come off the top of the preacher's head. The result of insufficient preparation is a presentation which bears no resemblance to the manner of preaching and teaching which we find in the Bible, particularly in the gospels. Without sufficient preparation the preaching of God's word is not efficacious but empty, not sharp but dull, not living but dead.

The sermons of Jesus are not abstract. They are concrete and specific. Much the same can be said for the rest of the Bible. St. Paul's letters are in some instances thought of as being somewhat abstruse. They are profound but they too make use of the forms of support and are not mere assertions. An assertion is a message which is in an inadequate medium. Frequently an unprepared homily is little more than a tissue of assertions without adequate support. It also happens that when a preacher is told that he must stick to one central idea, he is at a loss as to how to do anything except state the idea. He worries about how he will "fill out the time" if he is not allowed to present three or more points. Proper support does more than fill out the time. It makes an assertion effective and memorable.

An assertion can be supported in any of several ways which are known as the Forms of Support. One of the principal burdens of composition is to find appropriate Forms of Support. Although the term, Support, may suggest proof, it should be kept in mind that the nature of supporting material is to be determined by the General End. When the General End is Clearness, supporting material should be clarifying. When the End is Impression, supporting material should have emotional appeal. When the General End is Action, it should be motivating. Only when the General End is Persuasion is supporting material related to proof. (The four General Ends will be treated in Chapters VII and VIII.) The following are considered the usual or common Forms of Support.

Restatement

Restatement uses two or more equivalent expressions. It presents the idea "in other words." An example is: "Christianity is not a religion of faith alone. If our belief does not affect our conduct, we are not faithful followers of Christ. Faith without good works is dead." Jesus used Restatement when he promised the Eucharist: "Let me solemnly assure you, if you do not eat the flesh of the Son of man and drink his blood, you have no life in you. He who feeds on my flesh and drinks my blood has life eternal, and I will raise him up on the last day" (Jn 6:53-54). In two verses Jesus said essentially the same thing twice. A preacher must realize that people do not hear every word he says. They miss parts of the homily sometimes because of disturbances around them, sometimes because of mental distractions. That is when restatement may be used, but it should be reserved for the support of a central or critical idea. A common mistake of an unprepared preacher is to repeat an idea needlessly. He is not sure that he has made his point because he is really not sure what his point is, or he has not prepared sufficiently so that he may express his idea adequately in a few words.

Analogy and Metaphors

Jesus loved analogies and metaphors. That is why he asked himself while preparing to preach, "What is the kingdom of heaven like? To what shall I compare it?" Analogy is based on the principle that we proceed from the known to the unknown. It points out the similarities between what is already understood, appreciated, persuasive, or evident and what is not. An analogy makes an explicit comparison: "The kingdom of heaven is like a dragnet thrown into the sea." A metaphor makes only an implicit comparison, as when Jesus said, "I am the light of the world."

My father was a man of one sport. He loved baseball. In his old age (he lived to be 95) I tried to get him interested in football so that he would have a sport to follow when baseball was not in season, but it simply was not his game. He once asked me, "What is a first down in football? Is it like a hit in baseball?" He was doing by instinct what a preacher should do by design: trying to find a point of comparison in order to go from the known to the unknown.

Read again the "Sermon on the Mount" in the fifth, sixth, and seventh chapters of St. Matthew's gospel. It is filled with analogies and metaphors: the salt of the earth, the light of the world, the heavenly treasure, the birds of the sky, the wild flowers, the speck in the eye, the narrow gate, false prophets in sheep's clothing, the fruit of the tree, the house built on rock. In the thirteenth chapter of St. Matthew's gospel Jesus says that the kingdom of heaven is like a man who sells all that he has to buy a field in which a treasure is buried. It is like a merchant's search for fine pearls. These are only some of the analogies in the gospels.

The epistles too make use of analogies. When St. Paul was confronted with the petty jealousies and rivalries of his converts at Corinth, he compared the Church to a human body in which all the parts work for the good of the whole body (see 1 Cor 12). That analogy is so powerful that the Church has developed it in to the doctrine of the Mystical Body of Christ. This doctrine is in turn supported by the analogy of the Vine and the Branches in the fifteenth chapter of St. John's gospel.

Analogies must be drawn from the experience of the people, not that of the preacher, or they must be such that the audience can understand and appreciate them. A preacher once said that the happiness of heaven is everlasting, "not for an uncertain moment, trembling like quicksilver in my grasp." Since I have never held quicksilver in my hand, I did not find the analogy appealing or helpful. To find a proper analogy, ask yourself, "What is my idea like in the experiences of my audience?"

Illustration

Illustration is a favorite form of support. There are two characteristics of a good illustration. The first is that it is narrative in form; it tells a story. It has a plot, however brief, with a beginning, a middle, and an end. There are people or actors in the story who move the plot along or who are affected by the action. The second characteristic is that the details of the story are vividly described in order to make it interesting and visual. An illustration may be factual, such as the story of Jesus' visit to the home of Martha and Mary, or fictitious, such as the parable of the Good Samaritan. Factual or fictitious, an illustration is a medium in which is found a message which presents the truth.

Jesus told a brief parable which in only five verses exemplifies the principles of an effective illustration. It is the story of the Pharisee and the tax collector in Luke 18:10-14. As the plot begins two men begin to pray. In the middle of the plot one prays with pride, the other with humility. In the end God reacts. The message is that God is pleased with the humble man. Note the details which are not in my plot summary but which are in the parable. Jesus did not merely say that two men were praying. He placed them in the temple in order to set the scene. Then Jesus was not satisfied to say that one prayed with pride and the other with humility; he quoted what each man said in his prayer. He did not conclude with a general statement that one prayed well and the other prayed poorly. He was specific in his conclusion by stating that "this man went home from the temple justified while the other did not." (I am happy to give Jesus the grade of "A" for this illustration.)

Think of how memorable are the parables of Jesus, among which are such favorites as the Prodigal Son and the Good Samaritan. Actually the four gospels in their entirety are illustrations. For example, St. Luke is not satisfied to inform us that Jesus is compassionate; he tells us the story of the widow of Nain. That is one reason why the gospels have a greater appeal to most people than do the epistles. They tell the story of the good news, and everyone loves a good story.

Preachers must constantly be searching for appropriate illustrations, but they should also realize that illustration is only one form of support and need not be a component of every homily. In fact, the homilist must guard against becoming predictable. If a preacher always begins with a story, the people may learn to listen to the story and to lapse into inattention during the rest of the homily.

Allegory

Analogies, metaphors, and illustrations are sometimes allegorical or can be made to be so. Allegory extends the significance of these forms of support so that there is a step by step comparison. Some of the parables of Jesus are "pure" parables and others are at least partly allegorical. In a pure parable the details paint a vivid picture in order to hold attention but the story has only a single point. For instance, Jesus told the brief story of a man who goes to his friend in the middle of the night to ask for food so that he may feed an unexpected guest. His friend resents the fact that he has been awakened from a sound sleep. At first he refuses to help, but because the man persists he gives him what he wants (Seventeenth Sunday of the Year, C). When people do not understand a pure parable and begin to treat it allegorically, some details become noise factors. In hearing this parable someone may think, "What a strange picture of God — asleep and resistant." But the man in bed does not represent God. Jesus himself tells us that the point is found in one word: persistence. The message is that when you pray, you must never give up. This is a pure parable.

Some parables are partly allegorical. It is quite proper in the parable of the prodigal son to recognize that the younger son represents the tax collectors and sinners, that the older son represents the Pharisees and scribes, and that the father represents God. It is useless, however, to speculate on the symbolism of the inheritance or the "distant land" where the boy squandered the money. Scripture scholars caution us not to let our imaginations run wild in listening to parables (even though it can be fun to do so) since we should not invent meanings which the scriptures do not intend.

Specific Instances

A specific instance is a condensed form of the illustration. It is an abbreviated story, factual or fictitious. It is an example which makes an assertion concrete. A specific instance may be used as a medium when there is not sufficient time for an illustration. Sometimes several specific instances are helpful in order to develop an idea or to appeal to different people within the congregation. When I am listening to a homily I often find myself mentally calling out to the homilist, "For instance?" or "For example?" If he responds to my wish for him to be concrete, he is using specific instance.

The Fourth Eucharistic Prayer employs specific instances. The assertion is: "Father, we acknowledge your greatness: all your actions show your wisdom and love." I immediately want to ask, "For example? What are some specific instances of God's wisdom and love?" The prayer proceeds with those specific instances about creation, the covenant, the promises of the prophets, the incarnation, the birth of Jesus, his public ministry, and his paschal mystery. Notice that these specific instances are narrative in form, as are illustrations: "... You sent your only Son to be our Savior. To the poor he proclaimed the good news...."

Jesus used specific instances. In preaching the loving response of God to prayers of petition Jesus made the assertion, "If you, with all your sins, know how to give your children good things, how much more will the heavenly Father give the Holy Spirit to those who ask him." He wanted to support his assertion by a means of specific instance, and so he asked rhetorically, "What father among you will give his son a snake if he asks for a fish, or hand him a scorpion if he asks for an egg?" This specific instance contains a latent illustration which Jesus could have presented this way: "A little boy had been playing all day and was tired and hungry. He saw his father coming home from work and ran to meet him. He cried out,

'Daddy, I've been having a lot of fun and, boy, am I starved! Do we have anything to eat?' His father smiled and swept the boy into his arms and said, 'Let's go in the house and see what your mother has on hand.' I ask you, what kind of a father would this man be if, instead of taking his little boy into the kitchen, he had led him around to the back of the house where from the weeds he picked up a snake and thrust it at his child? Good parents do not do that kind of thing. Remember, then, that God is more loving than even the best of all human parents." Jesus reduced that illustration to a specific instance.

Statistics

The usual complaint against statistics is that they can be manipulated to prove anything. Disraeli made the famous statement: "There are lies, damn lies, and statistics." One fact about statistics is that they are usually boring. Numbers by themselves are abstract. If they are to be used, they should be made vivid by comparison with things which are familiar, or by being put into a dramatic setting. I have no realization of what a million dollars is, let alone a billion. The difference was impressed upon me by this illustration. "A wealthy man gave his son a million dollars and told him to go out and spend a thousand dollars a day. He was to return to his father when he had run out of money and to ask for more. He did as he was directed and returned after three years, having spent the million. His father then gave him a billion dollars and told him to go and spend a thousand dollars a day and to return when he had run out of money. The boy did not return for three thousand years." That shows the difference between a million and a billion. (It also helps to put our national debt into perspective.)

I know that there is a shortage of priests in the United States, including the largest archdiocese in the country, Los Angeles. I did not realize how serious the shortage is until someone used statistics effectively: "If every Catholic in Los Angeles wanted to go to confession before Easter, it would take all the available priests seventy-five hours each to accomplish the task at only three minutes for a confession. In other words, each priest would have to spend almost ten days at eight-hours a day doing nothing other than hearing confessions."

Jesus used statistics, or at least numbers, on a few occasions. He once said to his disciples: "Are not two sparrows sold for next to nothing? Yet not a single sparrow falls to the ground without your Father's consent. As for you, every hair on your head has been counted; so do not be afraid of anything. You are worth more than an entire flock of sparrows" (Mt 10:29-31). On another occasion he said, "If a king is about to march on another king to do battle with him, will he not sit down first and consider whether with ten thousand men, he can withstand an enemy coming against him with twenty thousand?" (Lk 14:31). Statistics are not a common medium in homilies, but at times they can be effective if they are used with a little imagination.

Testimony

Testimony as a form of support relies on the statement or witness of someone other than the speaker. Quoting sacred scripture is using testimony. Referring to a teaching by an ecumenical council, by the Pope, one of the Fathers of the Church, a recognized theologian, or a saint is an appeal to testimony. When Jesus in the synagogue of Nazareth read the passage from Isaiah about the anointed of the Lord, he presented it as a testimony to his identity (Lk 4:14-21). He did something similar in answer to the question of the Baptist, "Are you 'He who is to come' or do we look for another?" (Mt 11:2 ff.). In St. John's gospel Jesus said, "It is laid down in your law that evidence given by two persons is valid. I am one of those testifying in my behalf, the Father who sent me is the other" (8:17-18).

When considering the use of testimony ask yourself these questions: 1) Have I properly identified the witness? 2) Is the witness an expert in the subject? 3) Is his opinion influenced by personal interest or is he objective? 4) Will the audience accept him? In using testimony the speaker says, "Don't take my word for it. Listen to what an expert has to say."

Visualization

We live in a society which has become used to visual presentations, and not merely verbal ones, because of movies and television. Pictures, however, can be painted with words. When they are, the process is called Visualization. It is not precisely a separate form of support; rather it is a quality which enhances every form of support.

Listen aloud to the following periodic sentence, which I consider to be perfect in its construction, and allow your imagination to paint the scene: "During the whole of a dull, dark, and soundless day in the autumn of the year, when the clouds hung oppressively low in the heavens, I had been passing alone on horseback through a singularly dreary tract of country and at length found myself, as the shades of the evening drew on, within view of the melancholy house of Usher." The literary style of this periodic sentence is not appropriate for the spoken style, but the visualization created by Edgar Allen Poe in this first sentence of his short story, "The Fall of the House of Usher," can be achieved in simpler sentences which are suited to the spoken style. According to Sylvester MacNutt, formerly a professor of homiletics, an Arabian proverb states that "a great orator turns his listeners' ears into eyes."

A preacher who has not prepared his homily well might

say: "A woman who loses a coin searches for it until she happily finds it." Instead Jesus painted a picture: "What woman, if she has ten silver pieces and loses one, does not light a lamp and sweep the house in a diligent search until she has retrieved what she lost? And when she finds it, she calls in her friends and neighbors to say, 'Rejoice with me! I have found the silver piece I lost'" (Lk 15:8-9).

An unprepared preacher might say, "A rich man completely ignored a beggar at his door." Jesus painted a picture: "Once there was a rich man who dressed in purple and linen and feasted splendidly every day. At his gate lay a beggar named Lazarus who was covered with sores" (Lk 16:19-21). Get the picture?

Some preachers implement the principle of visualization by using what we call visual aids. Although I personally prefer using words to paint pictures because they help the audience to use their imagination, there are precedents in the Bible for visual aids. See the first reading of the Mass for Friday of the Fifth Week of the Year from the First Book of Kings (11:29 ff.) in which the prophet Ahijah tore his cloak into twelve pieces and gave ten pieces to Jeroboam to visualize that Solomon's kingdom would be divided, ten tribes to the north and two to the south (Judah and Simeon). The prophets Ezekiel and Jeremiah both used visual aids. One example from Jeremiah is the use of the clay in the potter's hand to visualize how Israel was shaped by the Lord (see Thursday of the Seventeenth Week), but personally I prefer the verbal visualization of the dry bones in Ezekiel 37 (Friday of the Twentieth Week). Jeremiah's use of his loin cloth as a visual aid (on Monday of the Seventeen Week) was apparently acceptable in his day but it may strike us as not being in very good taste for an audience, and therefore a noise factor. To be effective visual aids must not only be in good taste but they must also be clear, easily seen by everyone, and ready to be used at the proper time. Laugh-

able or annoying are the results when the slide projector does
not work or a portrait is so small that it cannot be seen beyond
the first pew.

Supporting the Right Idea

Sometimes preachers develop the obvious. They support
the wrong idea. A preacher who wishes to teach that there are
many legitimate expressions of liturgy in the Church may
begin by observing that people have varied ways of looking at
reality and have different needs according to their background and their culture. Every person with even a little
experience in life knows that. The preacher need not give
many instances to exemplify that fact. He should spend his
time developing the assertion that liturgical expressions which
seem foreign to his listeners are appropriate forms of Catholic
worship.

Balance and Proportion

Some preachers get carried away with their illustrations
and their analogies. Their sermons are little more than a story
sometimes with a brief application, sometimes not. When this
approach is employed judiciously, the result can be dramatic
and effective, but if it is used regularly it becomes predictable
and often ineffective. In order to present doctrine effectively,
the preacher usually needs to apply his illustration or analogy
in a clear fashion. A fable, such as Aesop's story of the
shepherd boy who cried "Wolf, wolf," once too often needs no
more than the telling, but Christian revelation is more profound than this or any fable.

Supportive material should be in balance with the rest of
the homily. Sometimes an illustration may be out of balance by
taking up two thirds or three fourths of the time of the homily,
and yet it may be so powerful or so allegorical that it is in proper

proportion. When Jesus had concluded the parable of the Good Samaritan, he added only a sentence to express his point. When he told the parable of the servant who refused to be as forgiving as his master, he used only a few words for his application. Both parables lack balance but are properly proportionate.

Preparation

A large part of the time which is dedicated to homily preparation should be spent in developing proper forms of support. That requires imagination. Walt Disney referred to the creative aspect of his studio as "Imagineering." Preparing a homily is partly imagineering. When a homilist does not prepare properly, the message is presented in a medium which does not help the audience to develop the correct message.

SUMMARY:

Support is necessary to place the message in a proper medium. The usual forms of support are restatement, analogy, illustration, specific instance, testimony, and statistics. Analogies can be allegorized. All forms of support should be made mentally visual. There must be a balance between supporting material and the message in itself, or at least there should be an appropriate proportionality.

EXERCISE:

Go through the gospels and pick out some examples for each of the Forms of Support.

"Our public men are speaking everyday on something, but they ain't saying anything."

Will Rogers

CHAPTER VI

SELECTING THE MEDIUM: REFERENCES TO EXPERIENCE

"When the clouds are full, they pour out rain upon the earth." (Ec 11:3)

Some people have an image of a holy person. He is thin, almost emaciated. He kneels in the back of a dark church for long hours, his hands buried in his face. He seems far removed from the world in which ordinary people live. He is not interested in TV, movies, sports, or eating and drinking. He does not look at pretty women and he is reluctant to speak with them. He seems to want no friends. He is a somewhat solitary figure. He is thought of as a contemplative.

That may be one form of holiness, but if a priest follows it he will never preach the way Jesus did. In order to imitate Jesus as an effective preacher, one must be a contemplative of the human as well as the divine. One without the other is insufficient. Preachers who are not entirely imbued with the Word of God give sermons which are shallow, jejune, and humanistic. These sermons, which are hardly distinguishable from advise given in newspapers columns, are not the proclamation of the Word of God. It is not enough, however, for a preacher to know the Word of God; he must also know his people. A preacher who is not a student of people, their lives, and their circumstances gives sermons which are irrelevant, incomprehensible, and banal. When sermons are divorced from life, people hear them as pious prattle and nothing more. A priest must be a contemplative but not a hermit. He must fill himself not only with an understanding of God's word but with an appreciation of his people's experience. When his clouds are full, they pour forth the rain which waters the earth, making it fertile and fruitful.

While they are listening to a priest, some people conclude that he is very holy or very intelligent, but they have no idea of what his sermon is about. He has failed to put the message of God into a medium which reflects the experience of his people. People cannot understand us if we do not talk their language. People cannot derive meaning from the Word of God if we do not present it within the context of their lives. We must follow the principle which is called "Reference to Experience." This principle is the rhetorical corollary of the spiritual principle of Apostolic Praying (see Chapter III).

The principle of Reference to Experience is not concerned with the preacher's life but with that of his people. A priest may at times speak of what has happened to him, but such references are helpful only if people can identify with them. Even then, it is generally better if the priest relates his experiences as having happened to a third person, particularly when he may seem to come off as the hero. Remember the approach used by St. Paul in his Second Letter to the Corinthians: "I know a man in Christ who fourteen years ago... was snatched up to Paradise to hear words which cannot be uttered..." (12:2-4). The man was, of course, Paul himself. Nor does reference to experience mean that the priest makes a public confession of his sins from the pulpit. Such may seem humble and honest, but it is usually quite inappropriate.

It happens not infrequently that a preacher who thinks in terms of people's lives can express for them what they already believe and know, but for which they do not have the words or images. A happy reaction of an audience is, "Yes, that's the way it is," or "I knew that but I could not express it," or "I had not thought of it in exactly that way but what you say makes a lot of sense to me."

Using references to experience is another way of imitating the way Jesus preached. It is to preach New Testament Style. When Jesus called the first apostles (as related in Mt 4:18 ff.), even though, we presume, he had been a carpenter with Joseph at Nazareth, he did not say, "Come after me and I will make you carpenters to build my Church." He spoke in terms of their livelihood, not his own, and said, "Come after me and I will make you fishers of men."

Though he was not a farmer, Jesus talked about planting seeds. Though he was not a soldier, he spoke of going to war. Though he was not married, he referred to weddings banquets as frequently as if he were the father of many daughters. Though he was a male, he used a female image to illustrate that the sorrow of his death would be turned into the joy of his resurrection: he said that a woman is in sorrow when her time has come for delivering her baby, but once the baby has been born she no longer remembers her pain because of her joy that a child has been born into the world.

Jesus referred to current events. A good example is the gospel for the Third Sunday of Lent in Cycle C. Some people gave Jesus tragic news about Galileans "whose blood Pilate had mixed with their sacrifices." He said in reply, "Do you think that these Galileans were the greatest sinners in Galilee just be cause they suffered this? By no means! But I tell you, you will all come to the same end unless you reform." Then Jesus referred to another tragedy which apparently his audience had heard about: "Or take those eighteen who were killed by a falling tower in Siloam. Do you think that they were more guilty than anyone else who lives in Jerusalem? But I tell you, you will all come to the same end unless you begin to reform."

When Jesus told the story of the Good Samaritan, he did not speak in generalities by saying that a man on a journey was robbed. He made a reference to the lives of his listeners by beginning the story in this way: "There was a man going down from Jerusalem to Jericho who fell in with robbers." Everyone in the crowd had gone along that road. It was so familiar to them that they saw a picture of it in their minds while Jesus spoke. In fact, the full effect of some of Jesus' teaching is lost on us simply because his approach was so well suited to the people to whom he preached and for whom the gospels were originally composed.

A preacher who is a contemplative of both God's word and God's people knows how to put God's message into a medium with which the people can identify. St. Paul realized that many of the people of Corinth were sports enthusiasts (does anything really change?), and so he reminded the Corinthians: "Athletes deny themselves all sorts of things. They do this to win a crown of leaves that withers, but we a crown that is imperishable" (1 Cor 9:25).

Some Examples of Reference to Experience

Preachers today must find their own references to experience. If I want to assert that the Church is more than a means for an individual to get to heaven, I need to support the assertion. To do so I may use the following extended analogy which employs a contemporary form of reference to experience:

"Some Catholics look upon the Church only as a way to get to heaven. They have little appreciation of the Church as the family of God into which they have been born through baptism and to which they have responsibilities. They believe that the only thing that counts is getting to their heavenly mansion. They admit that other people are headed there too, but they see no need to be involved with them. They have what I call 'elevator spirituality.' You may have noticed how rare it is for strangers on an elevator to speak to one another. The ascent is made in silence. All eyes are fixed on the little lights which indicate which floor the elevator is passing. In fact, it matters little to the person who wants to get to the top floor whether anyone else is in the elevator or not. He does not care about how the elevator works and he is unconcerned about what to do if something goes wrong. He simply wants to get to the top."

This extended analogy is based on the experience of riding in an elevator. It may also be made allegorical. For example, we could say that it is possible to get off before getting to the top in order to explore what is on the lower floors. Some people do that. They wander away from the Church, still thinking that they can always catch another elevator to the top before closing time. Another analogy can be used to offset elevator spirituality: "Christ is the Way to heaven, but he is inseparably linked to his people, somewhat like people who are climbing a mountain and who are tied by ropes to each other and through each other to the leader at the top." Within this analogy is the assertion that God calls for a cooperative effort of the people who make up the Church.

References to experience may be either direct or indirect. Direct experience is first hand. It includes all those things which people go through in their own immediate activity. Indirect experience is second hand or vicarious. For people who have been on an elevator, the analogy about the Church is a reference to direct experience. For people who have never been on an elevator, the analogy is a reference to indirect experience since they have at least seen people in an elevator in movies or on TV. References to direct experience are usually more effective than references to indirect experience.

Good references are found in experiences which are recent, or personal, or intense. The news on TV or in the paper is a form of recent, although vicarious, experience. An allusion to observing one's birthday is a reference to personal experience, and speaking of the death of a loved one is a reference to an intense experience. Helpful references are those which include experiences which happen frequently, such as going shopping or preparing meals, or which are readily remembered, such as a silver wedding jubilee or the birth of a first child.

A preacher who enjoyed mathematics tried to explain the Blessed Trinity by referring to the geometric fact that in a right-angled triangle the square of the hypotenuse is equal to the sum of the squares of the other two sides (why he did not refer to an equilateral triangle I do not know). That made sense to him but for most people it was a matter of going from the unknown to the unknown. His attempt was not a reference to experience. Someone once said that life without Christ would be like living at O'Hare airport in Chicago. If you have never been to O'Hare airport the reference means little to you, but if you have been through the experience of that confusing place, then the thought of it contains images of crowds, pushing and shoving, rushing back and forth in an impersonal environment in which everything has been reduced to numbers.

Some images need updating because they no longer reflect a contemporary experience. Psalm 78 laments the fact the people "strayed, as faithless as their fathers, like a bow on which the archer cannot count." That was a vivid image at the time the Psalm was composed, but I have never used a bow and arrow in all my life, and probably not many people have. I think instead of a jalopy, a car that is so unreliable that you never know whether it is going to start or not, especially on a cold morning. You can't count on it.

During the Mass on Tuesday of the Twelfth Week of the Year (II) Jesus tells us that we must "enter through the narrow gate. The door that leads to damnation is wide... but how narrow is the gate that leads to life...." Since I live in Southern California the image of the narrow gate makes me think of what happens on the freeway when there is a bad accident. The police close two or even three lanes; only a single lane is open which is like the narrow gate. All the traffic slows down and at times comes to a complete stop because of the bottleneck. As I think of the image which Jesus used, I see people all bunched up like cars on the freeway, moving very slowly, trying to squeeze through the one open lane. People are upset. They are fussing and fuming and being unkind to each other. Cars are overheating and everything is a mess. The bottleneck is actually a pain in the neck. Sin is like the accident on the freeway. That is what causes all our problems. It is not an inviting scene, this image of what it means to get to heaven. But when I think back to the image of the narrow gate, I remember that only one person has to get through that gate, and that person is Christ. Through the gate he has passed in the paschal mystery of his death and resurrection. We don't have to force our way through the narrow gate. All we need do is make sure we are united with Christ, especially through receiving the sacrament of the Eucharist, because many bodies do not have to squeeze through the gate, only one body, the Body of Christ.

This approach is based on references to experience. For people who live in an area where they are fortunate enough never to travel freeways, the reference to experience is indirect. To Southern Californians it is not only direct but intense and frequent. The mention of the passage of Jesus through the gate by means of his death and resurrection suggests the passage of God's people through the sea in the Exodus, a reference which will hit the mark depending on how filled the audience is with scriptural awareness.

Transcendent Meaning of Experience

The principle, Reference to Experience, and its helpmate, the Forms of Support, are based on the truth that God is consistent in his creation. Biologists, for example, observe that even though animals belong to different species they are

remarkably similar, not only in structure but more so in
function. A blue jay is very different from an African elephant,
and yet both have bodily parts in common, such as the head
which is the center of the senses, and similar functions, such
as digestion and reproduction. Despite their diversity, a blue
jay and an elephant admit of comparison. You can give a child
who has never seen an elephant some idea of that enormous
creature by comparing it with the tiny bird which the child
observes flying above him. (Someone might remark that it is
a good thing that only one of these two creatures can fly.)

When sound theology pervades our preaching, we make
a connection in faith between the natural and the supernatural, between the visible and the invisible. We acknowledge that
there is something of the supernatural in the natural, something of the invisible in the visible. God who is invisible and
spiritual is present and available to us through the visible and
material.

The Book of Wisdom declares: "All men are by nature
foolish who are ignorant of God, and who from the good
things seen do not succeed in knowing him who is, and from
studying the works do not discern the artisan.... From the
greatness and the beauty of created things their original
author, by analogy, is seen" (13:1 and 5).

We do not live in two worlds, one religious and one
secular. We live in God's world. That is our Catholic principle
of sacramentality. We see a person immersed in the waters of
baptism and we believe what we do not see, that he has been
plunged into the death of Christ. We see that same person
emerge from the water, and we believe what we do not see, that
he has been raised with Christ (Rm 6:3 ff.).

Jesus had no problem finding an analogy for the paschal
mystery. When he wanted to teach that we must lose our life to
save it, that we must die in order to live, he referred to what we
can observe in nature: "I solemnly assure you, unless the grain
of wheat falls to the earth and dies, it remains just a grain of

wheat. But if it dies, it produces much fruit" (Jn 12:24 ff.). St. Paul, treating our resurrection from the dead, wrote in a similar vein to the Corinthians: "Perhaps someone will say, 'How are the dead to be raised up? What kind of body will they have?' A nonsensical question! The seed you sow does not germinate unless it dies. When you sow, you do not sow the full-blown plant, but a kernel of wheat or some other grain. God gives the body to it as he pleases — to each seed its own fruition" (1 Cor 15:35 ff.).

Jesus, Master of Human Experience

Jesus was the master observer of human experience. He graced the wedding feast of Cana with his presence, and we may rightly conclude that he participated regularly in the celebration of marriages while he was growing up in Nazareth. I imagine that Mary and Joseph insisted on that just as parents do with their children today in similar circumstances. From these human events he drew material for his parables about wedding feasts, not merely because weddings reminded him of the relationship between God and his people, but because there is something of that divine relationship within the human relationship.

Early Jewish scholars debated whether "The Song of Songs," also known as "The Canticle of Canticles," should be part of the canonical scriptures. This book has nothing to do with sacred history, the law, or the covenant. In fact, it seems to be little more than a somewhat disconnected collection of popular love songs which do not even mention God. Around the year 90 A.D. the rabbis accepted the book because of the interpretation that it reflects the marriage of the Lord to his chosen people. The principle of sacramentality helps us to understand on another level why the book is canonical. In human love there is something of divine love because the divine is the source of the human, and the divine is manifested and experienced through the human. Jesus lived with an awareness that the world belongs to his Father, and preachers must do the same.

Jesus seems never to have refused an invitation to dinner. When he was coming to the end of his life on this earth, he wanted to have a meal with his disciples, to share the Passover supper for the last time. He did not have to search his imagination to discover appropriate signs for the sacrament of the Eucharist. He not only had them at hand during the supper in the bread and the wine, but all during his life he had experienced the nourishing and happy effects of eating and drinking with people. Of profound significance for him were the words of Ecclesiastes: "Go, eat your bread with joy and drink your wine with a merry heart, because it is now that God favors your works" (9:7). Jesus chose bread and wine for the Eucharist, not merely because they made him think of what he wanted to accomplish through the Eucharist, but because the human experience of dining together contains something of the divine experience of sharing in the eucharistic banquet. Msgr. Ronald Knox in his sermon, "Real Bread," suggested the idea that God did not design the Eucharist to be something like bread, simply because bread came first in time, but that he designed bread to be something like the Eucharist, because the Eucharist came first in his intention (an idea which, I suppose, can neither be proved nor disproved).

The principle of Reference to Experience in preaching, then, is based on what we understand through our theology of sacramentality. God is disclosed through signs. Jesus is the great sacrament of the Father's presence and action in our world, and the Church, which is Christ extended in space and time, is the universal sacrament of salvation. Actually all of God's creation is in some way his sacrament.

A Liturgical Example

For those who love the liturgy, Advent has a profound meaning. The reason is that it clearly reflects the human experience of happy anticipation. Advent is not an invention of the Church to arouse certain sentiments within us. Rather Advent came to be because the Church recognized instincts which God has placed within the human heart to correspond to the events of our salvation. Advent is the excitement of a child on his way to Disneyland for the first time who keeps begging his father, "Are we there yet, Daddy?" Advent is the conviction that something better is around the corner, that something wonderful is about to turn up. Advent is the search to find a lost feeling of love and to brighten faded memories of happier days. These simple but significant human sentiments are not divorced from faith, but are the raw materials from which are formed the most devout of religious aspirations. Advent helps us to realize that there is no reason to separate religion from life, and that there is every reason to relate human experience to the divine.

A Sense of Celebration

Before Vatican II we used varied verbs to express our relationship to the Mass. We spoke of a priest as saying Mass and of ourselves as hearing Mass. The Daughter of Charity who taught me in parochial school would ask on Monday morning, "Did you go to Mass yesterday?" I learned in the 1930's that Pope Pius XI was urging us to pray the Mass, and in the 1940's I read that Pope Pius XII taught us to offer the Mass. All of these verbs have a legitimate meaning, but in the liturgical restoration which is being brought about through the work of Vatican II we use still another verb to indicate our participation in the Eucharist, and that verb is "to celebrate."

Celebration is a joyful experience. You cannot imagine a

family celebrating the tragic, premature death of the oldest son, killed in a violent automobile accident. And yet as Catholics we celebrate the death of Jesus Christ. We call the day on which he died "good," because the death of Jesus was not tragic, premature, or accidental. It was the fulfillment of his purpose in becoming human. By dying he destroyed our death and by rising he restored our life, and he has thereby made us God's holy people. In the holy Eucharist we celebrate his death and resurrection.

Celebration is something you never do alone. Feeling lost in a strange city all by yourself, you would not really be able to celebrate your birthday. Celebrations are festive, and they involve people. They also include music, food and drink, often gift giving, and at times a person stands up, offers a toast, and gives a speech about the meaning of the celebration. These are elements of liturgy because by God's design human celebration contains some of the significance of sacred celebration. Human celebration has a transcendent meaning.

Is All Reality Transcendent?

I am not sure whether all analogies or illustrations which are references to experience are based on the transcendent meaning of human living. Is there really a transcendent meaning about God's kingdom in the fact that a net cast into the sea will bring up both good and bad fish, or is there a mere similarity? Maybe we must constantly struggle to find the deeper aspects of ordinary things. At one time I thought the only way I could pray Psalm 45 about the marriage of an Israelite king to a foreign princess was by imagining that the king represented Christ and that the princess represented the Church. Now I believe in the transcendent meaning of that wedding.

St. Vincent Ferrer in his treatise "On the Spiritual Life" wrote: "When you treat virtuous and sinful acts in your sermons and exhortations, use simple language and sensible idioms. Give apt and precise examples whenever you can. Each sinner in your congregation should feel moved as though you were preaching to him alone. Your words should sound as though they were coming, not from a proud or angry soul, but from a charitable and loving heart. Your tone of voice should be that of a father who suffers with his sinful children, as though they were seriously ill or were lying in a huge pit, and he struggles to free them, raise them up, and cherish them like a mother, as one who is happy over their progress and the hope they have of heaven's glory. This way of preaching has proven profitable to congregations; an abstract discourse on the virtues and vices hardly inspires those who listen" (See Office of Readings for April 5).

I think that every preacher must constantly search for all forms of support, transcendent or not, but I am also convinced that we need to continue the effort to develop our homiletic spirituality, to be contemplatives of human experience. We must attempt to preach in the manner of Jesus, New Testament Style.

SUMMARY:

A preacher must be a contemplative, not only of God's word, but of human experience. He must have homiletic spirituality, which is an "open-eyed" spirituality. We do not live in two worlds, one religious and one secular. We live in God's world.

EXERCISE:

Select some references to experience which you think Jesus would use in preaching today.

*"What orators lack in depth,
they make up to you in length."*
Baron de La Brede et de Montesquieu

CHAPTER VII

REFINING THE MEDIUM: UNITY AND COHERENCE

"Like a wise man be brief, but say much in a few words." (Si 32:8)

Hard work is required to achieve the unity and coherence which are necessary to make a homily effective. We need prayer, study, and reflection, but these are not a substitute for discipline. Some preachers seem to feel that if you throw enough mud at the wall, some of it is bound to stick, but the only result of throwing mud at a wall is a muddy wall. Homilies which contain many ideas can be so muddy that the congregation has no idea of what the homilist is speaking about. John Henry Newman wrote in *The Idea of a University* that "Nothing is so fatal to the effect of a sermon as the habit of preaching on three or four subjects at once" (p. 412). In order to achieve unity and coherence, you must go through several steps.

The Audience

After determining the message or topic, the first step in homiletic composition is to think about the audience. In this context I prefer the word "audience" to "congregation" or "assembly" because of its etymology from the Latin verb "to hear." The people for whom the homily is intended are hearers; they are listeners. "Faith comes by hearing" (Rm 10:17).

The effort to know your people, their needs and frustrations, their convictions and doubts, their prejudices and their openness, is essential to effective preaching. A priest I know insists that when his mother was in a Catholic nursing home, the celebrant of a Sunday Mass preached a sermon to the sisters and their elderly patients (most of the latter attended the Mass in wheelchairs) on the evils of artificial birth control. That is, of course, an extreme example, but no less appropriate is a sermon on the sin of neglecting the poor to people whose parish is so destitute that it has to be subsidized by the diocese.

Not only must you make an effort to know your people well, but you must realize that it is an effort which has to be continually renewed. Nothing is static these days, least of all the specific needs and problems of people.

The Occasion

Circumstances should color what you have to say. On an Easter Sunday, a certain priest preached a very beautiful, well composed, well delivered sermon. It did not go over with the people. For some unaccountable reason he chose to preach exclusively on the mental sufferings of Christ in His agony. The subject simply was not suited to the occasion.

In 1968 Trinity Sunday fell on June 2nd, just four days after Senator Robert Kennedy had died from an assassin's bullet. The day had been proclaimed one of national mourning by President Johnson. At the Masses I celebrated I had to sit, as did the people, and listen to a missionary deliver an appeal for a diocese in Africa. People after the Mass told me that they hardly heard what the missionary had to say. The subject and especially the way in which it had been treated were too far removed from the occasion and the thoughts in their minds. Granted that the appeal could not have been delayed, the preacher would have done much better if he had pointed out that the real tragedy was not only that a Senator had been shot, not principally that a presidential candidate had been cut down. The real tragedy was that the dignity of a human person, created in the image of the Trinity and baptized in the name of the Father and the Son and the Holy Spirit, had been violated. Then he could have observed that the missionaries, out of respect and concern for the value of a human person, are attempting to give people a share in the blessings of faith which lead to the fullness of life in God. Contributions to the missions, he could have pointed out, are a definite way of recognizing the importance of human persons and a positive antidote to the poison of disrespect and disregard that so abruptly terminated the life of Senator Kennedy. Such an approach would have had more appeal than the most moving sermon which ignored the occasion.

On May 3 one year a preacher presented a complete exegesis on the scripture readings, which were from First Corinthians (15:1-8) and the gospel according to John (14:6-14). May 3 is the Feast of Saints Philip and James. The reason these readings were selected is that James is mentioned in the first reading and Philip in the gospel, and yet the preacher did not even allude to these apostles in his sermon. He had neglected the occasion.

In thinking about the occasion, you must take into consideration such things as the hour of the day, the nature of the setting, and the purpose of the liturgical celebration, but above all you must attempt to discern the thoughts that are uppermost at the moment in the minds of the people.

The Time Limit

In almost every parish there is the problem of not enough time for the Sunday celebration. You have to get the people out of one Mass promptly so that others can get in for the next Mass without chaos in the parking lot. Moreover, Americans are acutely aware of how long they are kept in church. I would say that normally for most people not much more than fifty or fifty-five minutes on Sunday is about the maximum of their tolerance, no matter how beautifully the Mass is celebrated or how eloquently the sermon is preached. Under these circumstances your homily can be only about ten minutes, depending too on the type of music, the number of communions, and the length of the announcements. As a matter of principle, you should aim to make your homily seven minutes in length. At least, the preacher should follow this advice: "If after ten minutes you fail to strike oil, stop boring."

Weekdays present an even greater problem of time. Most people at a weekday celebration are on a tight schedule, and many of them must go directly from church to work. Preaching too long on a weekday can discourage people from coming. At the most you should preach for only three minutes on a weekday, and you would do better to aim at two. Limiting the time of the homily can be achieved with the proper approach and preparation, as we shall see later.

Lengthy homilies not only cause practical problems in a crowded schedule; more seriously they violate the nature of the liturgy. Our liturgy is balanced between word and sacrament. This does not mean that the Liturgy of the Word and the Liturgy of the Eucharist share equal time, but it does mean that we do not rush through the Liturgy of the Eucharist as if it were merely tacked on to scripture readings and a very long homily. Despite the importance of preaching, Catholic liturgy does not envision the sermon or homily as the most important, or the most lengthy, part of the service. A Spanish proverb says, "That which is brief, if it be good, is good twice over." Pete Wilson's father adds that "Words to be immortal need not be eternal."

Your Ability

It may seem like observing the obvious to say that you should choose a subject in accord with your own ability, but I have found that many preachers do not give enough thought to this element. Let us say that two subjects are validly derived from the message of the scripture readings. The people have a greater need to hear the first, but you judge that you are, at the present at least, not really prepared to cover it well. The people can benefit from the second subject which you can present well, even though it may not be quite as vital to them as the first. Choose the second subject. Of course, you should resolve to do some study on the first subject so that you may be able to preach it at another time.

When you have chosen a subject suited to your people, the occasion, the time allowed, and your own ability, you have made a good start in homiletic composition. But more discipline is needed. About any good topic there is always too much to say. The temptation is to start with the topic and then just say everything about it that you know. The result is usually confusion in the minds of your people and a sermon that is long and boring. After you have selected a subject suited to your people, the occasion, the time allowed, and your ability, you must begin to choose and organize your material. A preacher must have the humility to see that his ideas are not so wonderful that they must all be expressed to the full, and he must have discipline to restrict himself to one idea. There are definite steps to follow in order to achieve unity and coherence in a homily which is within a proper time limit. These steps are selecting the General End, the Statement of Aim, and the Central Idea.

1. The General End

As you sit down to prepare your sermon ask yourself the question, "Which general response do I want from the people concerning this subject?" You may feel that your people really need to understand something about the subject; you want to make something clear to them. On the other hand, you may judge that it is not a question of understanding; they know the basic doctrine, but they simply are not impressed by it; they do not have a deep feeling or appreciation. Thirdly, it may be that they are not convinced about a truth; they need to be persuaded about something. Finally you may see that the problem is not a lack of understanding or appreciation or persuasion but action; the people need to do something. The four basic responses, then, that you may elicit from the people are understanding, impression, persuasion, and action. Each of these responses is designated by a technical term called The General End. In summary form the general ends look like this:

1. CLEARNESS: I want the people to *understand* something.

2. IMPRESSION: I want the people to *feel* or *appreciate* something.

3. PERSUASION: I want the people to *believe* or be *convinced* of something.

4. ACTION: I want the people to *do* something.

These terms designate ends, not means. Sometimes a preacher must feel that he requires two categories, say both Impression and Action. His judgment is that people need to be impressed with the seriousness of the debt in a parish before they will contribute more money. He may use elements of impression in his homily but he is using them as a means; he still has one General End, which is action. Having two distinct General Ends in a homily simply does not work.

2. Specific End, The Statement of Aim

Once you have settled upon your General End, you can arrive at your Specific End or Statement of Aim. The Statement of Aim contains the Message. Obviously it is not practical to allow your Message to remain in general terms. Ask yourself the question, "Which particular or specific response do I want from the people?" If your general end is Clearness, the question is "What do I want the people to understand?" If the General End is Impression, the question is, "What do I want the people to feel or appreciate?" If the General End is Persuasion, the question is "What do I want the people to accept or believe?" If the General End is Action, the question is, "What do I want the people to do?" In other words, the Statement of Aim is a particularization of the General End. It is not general; it is specific. And it must be in harmony with the General End. To say that the General End is Clearness and to have an Aim which is concerned with Action manifests scattered thinking on the part of the homilist.

The Statement of Aim is for your benefit as a homilist. It helps you to make very certain in your own mind exactly what you want to accomplish. It is your precise purpose expressed in a complete sentence. Since it is for your benefit, it may be phrased in theological terminology. It always begins, "I want my audience to...." For example, with the General End of Clearness, a Statement of Aim could be: "I want my audience to understand that the sacrament of Penance is a sign of God's mercy, not his wrath." With the General End of Impression: "I want my audience to realize that sacrament of Penance manifests that in God's eyes they are more precious than a lost sheep is to a shepherd." With the General End of Persuasion: "I want my audience to accept that the sacrament of Penance is in accord with human needs." With the General End of Action: "I want the audience to come to the communal celebration of the sacrament of Penance as a preparation for Easter."

The Statement of Aim is expressed in terms of outcome by the audience, not in terms of the intention of the preacher. Not: "I want to make it clear that the only way we can be holy is to be dedicated to God`s will." Rather: "I want my audience to understand that the only way to be holy is to be dedicated to God`s will." The difference is not small. The first Statement of Aim centers on the preacher, but the second immediately turns to the audience.

3. The Central Idea

When you have formulated your desired response in the words of your Statement of Aim, you are ready to ask the question, "Why do I not have the response now that I wish?" Looking at the examples I have given of four Statements of Aim, you can ask a question regarding each: Why do people have a negative idea of the Sacrament of Penance and fail to understand its beautiful sign of God's loving mercy? Why do people have a poor sense of self-esteem and see themselves as worthless? Why do people think that the sacrament is not practical? Why do people fail to come to the communal celebration of Penance during Lent?

For each question you probably can come up with several answers, maybe many. Examine them for a common denominator or single idea that runs through all of them. It may be necessary to discard some of the answers, perhaps most, because they are separate and distinct. Keep thinking about the matter until you arrive at one idea which you can express in a sentence. This sentence is your Central Idea. You make use of this Idea to win the response which you have formulated in your Statement of Aim. It is an idea, the acceptance of which will attain the purpose of your homily. It is the point of unity, the whole homily in one sentence. Everything you say flows from it and converges upon it. It is the criterion for determining both what you should include in your homily and what you should exclude. The Central Idea is related to your Medium.

Looking again at the four Statements of Aim regarding the sacrament of Penance, I can suggest respective Central Ideas. For the first: "In this sacrament God reaches out, not to punish, but to forgive us." For the second: "God does not abandon us when we have sinned but out of love offers us the grace of repentance." For the third: "Our conviction that our sins are really forgiven is strengthened by the human elements of the sacrament." For the fourth: "We need to help and to pray for each other during the celebration of the sacrament."

The Statement of Aim is primarily for you, the homilist, and the Central Idea is primarily for your audience. The Statement of Aim leads the preacher to his Central Idea; the Central Idea leads the audience to the Statement of Aim. You want the people to hold onto the Central Idea after they have heard your homily. Above all, make sure that you have but a single idea. The homilist who states, "I have three points..." has failed to grasp the meaning and importance of the Central Idea.

Selecting and Following a Central Idea

Neglecting to formulate and follow a Central Idea, even though you have a precise Statement of Aim, results in a scattered, and often lengthy, presentation. Take the Seventh Sunday of the Year, Cycle B when the gospel is the story of the paralytic whose sins Jesus forgives (Mk 2:1-12). You determine that your General End is Clearness and your Statement of Aim is, "I want the audience to understand that the sacrament of Penance is a sign of God's mercy, not his wrath."

Maybe thinking about the sacrament of Penance leads you to reflect on how many people are afflicted with guilt and filled with shame from the time they were children. Then you reflect, on the other hand, that these days many people have no sense of guilt or shame because they have lost a recognition of sin. You remember, further, how many people have told you of their negative experiences with the sacrament because a priest bawled them out or told them they were going to hell or refused them absolution. Next you realize that some people object that they need not admit their sins to a man, even if he is a priest, since they can confess their sins directly to God. You wonder if maybe people have been scandalized by reports of child molestation by priests or by other shocking stories, and so have lost respect for the priesthood.

A priest who has not prepared adequately may actually try to cover all of these concepts. The result will be a long, rambling presentation in which no one idea is treated adequately, the very kind of homily people abhor. As a homilist you must face the fact that you cannot cover everything about a subject during a homily. The liturgy is not like going to school. You do not have the amount of time which you have during a class, you cannot field questions and allow discussion, nor can you demand that the people do assigned reading. Many facets of a topic may be treated in a class, but only one can be adequately presented in a homily (even, God forbid, a fifteen minute one). Accept the fact that you cannot do everything on one Sunday, but you do have fifty-two Sundays in a year. If you communicate a single idea each Sunday in an effective and memorable fashion, you will have, by God's grace, accomplished much.

And so returning to the homily on Penance and after having determined the message of the gospel about the paralyzed man, you might formulate this or a similar Central Idea: "In the sacrament of Penance Jesus is eager to forgive our sins with the same compassion he showed to the paralytic." Now you have something to work with. Since your General End is Clearness you can explain that Jesus acts through the priest, that he is the one who, using the voice of the priest, pronounces the beautiful words, "I absolve you from your sins." You think about the enemies of Jesus in this gospel. You recognize that they are a foil to Jesus, that they help us to see by their pettiness the bigness of Jesus in his mercy. You perceive that this thought contributes to your Central Idea about mercy. Then you reflect on how the friends of the paralytic helped him. At this point you are tempted to talk about how we ought to help each other to participate in the sacrament. It is a good thought but it is extraneous to your Central Idea. You correctly decide to leave it for another opportunity. That is how a Central Idea works.

President Calvin Coolidge was once asked, upon returning from church on Sunday, what the minister spoke about in his sermon. Laconic as always, he replied, "Sin." When he was then asked what the minister said about sin, he answered, "He was against it." He got the message. In contrast, a husband who had stayed home from church asked his wife what the priest preached about. She replied, "I don't know. He didn't say."

St. Luke in the tenth chapter of the Acts of the Apostles told the story of the conversion of Cornelius, a Roman centurion, and he gave us a good example of a Statement of Aim and a Central Idea. The General End of the story is Clearness. The Statement of Aim is: I want my audience "to see how true it is that God shows no partiality." The Central Idea is: "The man of any nation who fears God and acts uprightly is acceptable to him" (see Ac 10:34 ff.).

Transitions

A final but important means of unity, and particularly of coherence, is to employ good transitions. When you do not use good transitions, the audience begins asking at some point how you got from A to B, or sometimes from what seems to be from A to Z. If you started talking about the resurrection of Christ, they wonder why all of sudden you seem to be giving a history lesson on the Second World War. When you do use good transitions, the audience follows you across a clear, well lighted bridge. A transition, like a bridge which must touch both shores, has something of the previous thought within it and something of the thought to follow.

A frequent mistake is to fail to make a transition to an illustration or example. Think about the beginning of this homily for Thursday of the Thirteenth Week of Year I, the first reading for which is the story of Abraham's being asked to sacrifice his son, Isaac: "Faith means more than believing in God. Faith means turning one's whole life over to God with complete confidence. God made extraordinary promises to Abraham...." The audience protests, "Wait a minute. You were talking about faith and all of sudden you tell us that God made extraordinary promises to Abraham. Where does Abraham come in?" A simple transitional sentence would have made the presentation coherent and would have kept the audience listening: "Faith means turning one's whole life over to God with complete confidence. Abraham is the biblical man of faith. Through the gift of faith God had made extraordinary promises to him." The homily then goes on to show that Abraham's faith was so complete that he was willing to sacrifice his son. Transitions are the glue which holds the parts of the homily together after you have used all of the means for achieving unity.

Employing the means for unity is sometimes the hardest part of composition. When I am composing a homily, I enjoy searching for references to experience and forms of support. I love to mull over the liturgical scriptures and to do research on them in order to sift out the message. I like allowing all the ideas and images to bounce around in my head. But when it comes time to decide on a General End, to formulate a specific Statement of Aim, and to determine a precise Central Idea, I have to put on my work clothes and prepare to sweat a little. I may even have to shed some tears and a few drops of blood. All aspects of preparation involve hard work. This part of homi-letic preparation also requires relentless discipline. But nothing less than maximum effort is worthy of the privilege and duty of preaching. Even when we have done all that is necessary for homiletic preparation we should say "We are useless servants. We have done no more than our duty" (Lk 17:10).

SUMMARY:

Following a single General End gives unity and coherence to a homily. Each General End has its own elements.

EXERCISE:

Select a topic and do an outline of the elements for each of the four General Ends.

To preach or not to preach, that is not the question for a priest. Preaching is of the essence of being a priest.

CHAPTER VIII

THE FOUR GENERAL ENDS

"We proclaim the truth openly..." (2 Cor 4:2)

Experience shows that each General End has its own elements which make that End effective. These elements, it must be understood, are not steps to follow in order to organize a homily; rather, they are ingredients which combine to bring about the desired end.

A. *Clearness*

Clearness is the General End for an audience which does not understand the subject. The message to be presented, the truth to be understood, must be put into a medium which the audience can grasp. The procedure is simply to go from the known to the unknown. The first element of the General End of Clearness is called the Presentation. It is concrete, specific, and visual. The next element is Explanation. Its purpose is to elucidate, to elaborate, to exemplify the truth contained in the Presentation. The third element is Personal Implication. Truth has intrinsic value and yet it will be of concern to an audience only if they see its significance for themselves. That is why Personal Implication is one of the elements.

The scriptures present us with models of the General End of Clearness complete with the three elements. An example is

81

found in the discourse of Jesus at the Last Supper. On the night before he died Jesus wanted his disciples (statement of aim) to understand that they had to remain in union with him in order to lead the life of a disciple. In only eight verses St. John has left us a summary of the three elements Jesus used to make the truth clear (Jn 15:1-8). It is the allegory of the Vine and the Branches. Presentation: "I am the vine, you are the branches." Explanation: "Apart from me you can do nothing." Implication: "He who lives in me and I in him, will produce abundantly." The message from Jesus that apart from him disciples can do nothing is abstract. It was made concrete by the image of the vine and the branches. It was applied in the assertion that living in union with Jesus produces spiritual fruit. Each of these ingredients can be combined and developed into a complete homily, and I think they were by Jesus at the supper since what we have in the gospel is but a summary.

St. Paul employed the same ingredients when he was faced with divisions in the Church of Corinth because of envy and jealousy involving the spiritual gifts. The message he wanted to make clear was: "To each person the manifestation of the Spirit is given for the common good." To achieve this aim he used the analogy of the human body in his Presentation: "The Body is one and has many members, but all the members, many though they are, are one body." In his Explanation he made it clear that as the parts of a body work together for the good of the whole body, so do the gifts of the Spirit within the Church. The Personal Implication is: "You are the body of Christ. Every one of you is a member of it." (See 1 Cor 12:1-30).

The story of Joseph in the Old Testament (Gn 37-48) is a short story rather than a homily but it contains the same three elements of the General End of Clearness. The message of this story is that God brings good out of evil or, as it has often been expressed, "God writes straight with crooked lines."

The Presentation is the fascinating story of how Joseph

was sold into slavery by his brothers, how he was brought to Egypt and came to power so that he was able to help his father and his brothers during the years of famine. The Explanation is the episode in which Joseph revealed his identity to his brothers and told them "I am you brother Joseph, whom you once sold into Egypt. But now do not be distressed and do not reproach yourselves for having sold me here. It was really for the sake of saving lives that God sent me here ahead of you" (Gn 45:4-5). The Implication, though implicit, is clearly that God is not thwarted by evil in our lives, that for us too he can and does bring good out of evil.

The Third, Fourth, and Fifth Sundays of Lent in the A cycle contain gospels which are, in the patristic approach, Presentations on Christian Initiation. On the Third Sunday in the story of the Samaritan woman at Jacob's well, Jesus declared: "Whoever drinks the water I give will never be thirsty; no, the water I give shall become a fountain within him, leaping up to provide eternal life." The message is that the waters of baptism give the gift of everlasting life. On the Fourth Sunday in the story of the man who had been born blind, at the direction of Jesus the man went off and washed in the pool of Siloam and came back able to see. The message is that in the washing of baptism we are given faith, the gift of spiritual sight. On the Fifth Sunday in the story about Lazarus who had been dead for four days, Jesus declared, "I am the resurrection and the life." The message is that baptism is dying to sin and rising to new life in Christ. In each instance the homilist supplies the Explanation and the Implication.

An Example About Liturgy

Here is another example of the elements of Clearness. I think that some Catholics rejected the Second Vatican Council and its reforms because they had been taught that the Church could never change. That simplistic idea is the reason they were so shocked by the reform, especially by the liturgical restoration, and some have never really come to accept the changes except begrudgingly if at all. In speaking to these people I want them to understand something about the Church, particularly the Mass (General End of Clearness). I want them to understand that the Mass changes in accidentals but remains the same in essentials (Statement of Aim). My Central Idea is that because we are alive we change throughout the years and yet we remain the same person.

My Presentation briefly is this: When we were conceived in our mother's womb, we began life as a single cell. That cell multiplied and developed tissues and organs until we were ready to be born. Through infancy and childhood we grew into adulthood. What we are now is vastly different from what we were the day we were born, even more different from what we were when we were conceived, and yet through all the changes, some of them very significant, we remained the same person. Life demands these changes for the sake of growth. Through all our growth we changed in accidentals but re- mained the same in essentials. And that is the way it is with the Church and the Mass.

My Explanation briefly is this: The Mass is the supreme expression of what it means to be a Catholic. When Jesus instituted the Mass at the Last Supper, he spoke Aramaic, the simple form of Hebrew which he learned from Mary and Joseph at their home in Nazareth. As the Church began to grow beyond Jerusalem and Judea, the Mass was celebrated in Greek because it was the language that most people under- stood, even in Rome at the time St. Peter arrived there. In fact, all the Popes offered Mass in Greek until the beginning of the third century when Latin was introduced because most people no longer knew Greek. Many languages were used throughout the centuries, particularly in the Eastern Catholic Church, and now even in the Western Church the Mass is celebrated in the languages of the people. We have actually gone back to what

Jesus did, which is to use the language of everyday life. Language is accidental to the Mass. What is essential is to fulfill the command of Jesus, "Do this in memory of me." The Church during all its history has been faithful to this command. The Personal Implication is this: Our development from the moment of our conception was guided by the laws of nature which God has created. The development of the Mass and the changes by the Second Vatican Council have been guided by the Holy Spirit. As Catholics we embrace these changes so that we too may remain faithful to the command of Christ.

B. Impression

The General End of Impression is called for when an audience understands but fails to appreciate a message. The first element is Recognition. This is a minor element and it is needed only so that the preacher does not seem to be condescending. In every audience will be some sophomoric people who protest that they are always bored because they have heard it all before, but when everyone feels that way the preacher is in trouble. The element of Recognition lets the audience know that the preacher realizes that he is not saying something new to them. Recognition is accomplished by an attitude of the preacher more than by what he says, and yet at times some statement is helpful, such as "When we come to Mass on Sunday we can be pretty sure that we will often hear something in the scriptures about God's love for us, but we can never really comprehend the depth of this love."

As with the General End of Clearness, this End includes Personal Implication. The chief element, however, is Emotional Involvement, and that presents something of a problem. People of earlier generations, including priests, were warned that we must not trust our emotions, that feelings are hardly the solid foundation of authentic piety. The truth, of course, is more complex than we were led to believe. Feelings are important. Emotions are part of our human makeup. Values for many people are found, not in clear, precise reasoning, but in response to such realities as joy and sorrow, laughter and tears. Even if preachers recognize the importance of emotions, they may shy away from them in their homilies because there is less personal disclosure in distant, intellectual presentations than in those which reveal not only the mind of the preacher but his heart as well. Some are embarrassed to treat matters which may bring forth tears, either of happiness or sadness. And yet Jesus, since he was human like us in all things but sin, experienced our emotions. He wept over Jerusalem and he rejoiced that the Father had chosen to reveal himself to the little ones. Jesus showed his deep feelings for us when he said, "Come to me, all you who are weary and find life burdensome, and I will refresh you. Take my yoke upon your shoulders and learn from me that I am gentle and humble of heart" (Fourteenth Sunday of Year A). I think that Jesus was amused as he watched Zacchaeus climb a sycamore tree in order to see him (Thirty-First Sunday of Year C), and when he told Zacchaeus to hurry down I cannot imagine his doing so without a chuckle.

St. Luke in his seventh chapter lets us see a very tender side of Jesus (Tenth Sunday of the Year C). As he approached the town of Nain, "a dead man was being carried out, the only son of a widowed mother." I want to believe that at this touching moment Jesus in his mind saw his own widowed mother following the lifeless body of her only son to the tomb. It is no wonder that, as St. Luke observes for us, Jesus "was moved with pity at the sight of the woman." A similar compassion is revealed in the words of Jesus when during the sermon on the mount (Eighth Sunday of Year A) he urges us to stop worrying and says, "Your heavenly Father knows all that you need."

On the Twenty-Sixth Sunday of the Year C, we hear Jesus

tell the story of the rich man and Lazarus. He does so without hesitating to use emotional involvement: "Once there was a rich man who dressed in purple and linen and feasted splendidly each day. At his gate lay a beggar named Lazarus who was covered with sores. Lazarus longed to eat the scraps that fell from the rich man's table. The dogs even came and licked his sores." I think the only person not moved emotionally by this picture is someone who is as selfish as the rich man.

Everybody who watches football on TV has seen a fan at the game hold up a banner which reads, "John 3:16." The reference, of course, is to the sixteenth verse of the third chapter of the gospel according to John: "God so loved the world that he gave his only Son." I wish that these people would include the two previous verses: "Just as Moses lifted up the serpent in the desert, so must the Son of Man be lifted up that all who believe may have eternal life in him." These two verses help us to understand the meaning of John 3:16. It does not refer to the lovely star-bright night when Jesus was born in Bethlehem, but to the bleakness of Good Friday on Golgotha when Jesus was lifted up on the cross. When God "gave" his Son it was in the act of sacrifice. The cross reveals the depth of God's love for us and that realization can lead the preacher to the General End of Impression.

I grow in appreciating (General End of Impression) the significance of John 3:14-16 when I remember a little girl who had leukemia. She needed a bone transplant but her parents were not the proper match, nor was any adult who could be contacted. With the parents's permission, the doctor turned to the girl's younger brother. The doctor explained to the little boy, as best he could, that if his sister could not get the transplant she would die. The boy listened with his mouth open and his eyes wide. He swallowed hard and said he wanted to help his sister. The test showed compatibility and the transplant was effected. When it was over and a nurse inquired how he felt, he said that he was O.K. There was a pause before he asked in a small voice, "When do I die?" He thought that to save his sister's life, he had to give up his own. What he was willing to do, Jesus actually did so that we might not die but have eternal life.

Another important message of the gospel is Jesus' promise of eternal life which means that we are a pilgrim people. We are on a journey to heaven, our home. I love to hear Jesus say in the gospel of the Fifth Sunday of Easter in Year A: "Do not let your hearts be troubled... In my Father's house there are many dwelling places... I am going to prepare a place for you, and then I shall come back to take you with me." These are very consoling words from Jesus. I admit that I tend to forget them in times of discouragement, but the emotional involvement of the following illustration has helped me to appreciate Jesus' promise. A missionary had spent forty years in the Orient and was returning home to the United States to retire. On the airplane with him was a rock star who had just completed a two week tour. When they got off the plane in Los Angeles, a large crowd welcomed the rock star, but not one person was there to greet the missionary. He sighed and said, "Lord, here I have worked hard all these years for you in a foreign land and when I return there is no one to meet me even though there are hundreds to welcome home this entertainer." In a voice as quiet as a whisper the Lord said to him, "My son, you are not home yet."

C. Persuasion (Belief)

The General End of Persuasion is sometimes called Belief, but that designation can be confused with the belief of faith. Persuasion is the General End which is to be followed when it is necessary to move people from one conviction to another. Sometimes that involves faith, sometimes not. If you find it your duty to address members of the American Civil Liberties Union on the right of the unborn to life (good luck!), your General End would be Persuasion but this End would not involve faith for those who are not Catholics. If you had to convince reactionary Catholics of the authority of the Vatican Council, Persuasion would involve belief in the sense of faith. The chief element of this General End is the Point of Agreement which moves into the second element which is Continuous Assent.

An example of this General End is found in the follow-up to the familiar story of David and Bathsheba in the Second Book of Samuel (12:1-25). David committed adultery with Bathsheba and saw to the murder of her husband, Uriah. Nathan the prophet was sent by God to call David to repentance. Nathan was a wise man. He did not rush into the king's presence, shaking his finger in David's face and shrieking in the best fire and brimstone style, "You are guilty of adultery and murder!" That approach would probably have cost him his head. Instead he employed the General End of Persuasion and began with a Point of Agreement.

Very calmly he said to the king, "Judge this case for me. In a certain town there were two men, one rich and the other poor. The rich man had flocks and herds in great numbers. But the poor man had nothing at all except one little ewe lamb that he had bought. He nourished her and she grew up with him and his children. She shared the little food he had, and drank from his cup and slept in his bosom. She was like a daughter to him. Now, the rich man received a visitor, but he would not take from his own flocks and herds to prepare a meal for the wayfarer who had come to him. Instead he stole the poor man's ewe lamb and made a meal of it for his visitor." David took the bait. He grew angry and said in a tone of self-righteousness, "As the Lord lives, the man who has done this merits death! He shall restore the ewe lamb four-fold because he has done this and has had no pity." Nathan seized his opportunity and said to David, "You are the man!" Then he went on, using the element of Continuous Assent, to show the parallel between what David condemned in the rich man and what he himself had done to Uriah. It worked. With God's grace David repented.

When the General End is Persuasion, try to discover a point upon which you and your audience already agree and which is related to the position you want them to accept. You need a specific idea which is an application of a generic idea or principle. Find a specific idea which the audience does accept and which is related through the generic idea to what they do not as yet accept. Then show the parallel between what the audience already accepts and what they as yet do not accept. That is all rather abstract. I think the principle is clear when we remember what Nathan did. Nathan knew that David, despite his serious lapse, was a good, reasonable man, and that he would agree that it is despicable for a person who has plenty to take for his own use from a person who has little. Nathan expressed this generic idea in terms of the specific case of the rich man who stole the ewe lamb from the poor man. He then applied that specific case to what David had done. For another example of this approach from the Old Testament, try reading Isaiah 5:1-7.

Jesus employed this General End and established a point of agreement with the chief priests and elders of the people when he told the parable of the father who asked his two sons to work in his vineyard (Twenty-Sixth Sunday of the Year A). His audience agreed that the second son, who said he would not go but changed his mind and actually went into the vineyard, was the one who did what the father wanted. The truth which Jesus was teaching is that actions, not words, are obedience. He continued this approach in his next parable (Twenty-Seventh Sunday of the Year A) about the tenant farmers who mistreated all the slaves which the owner sent to collect his share of the harvest, and then killed the son whom the owner sent as a last resort. St. Matthew comments that the chief priests and the Pharisees realized that he was speaking about them, but apparently Jesus did not enjoy the kind of success which Nathan did by employing the General End of Persuasion, at least not immediately.

It can be very difficult to achieve the General End of Persuasion because it is often almost impossible to move people from one mindset to another. A preacher may have to be content with disturbing people who need to change their minds about something, of lessening their certainty, and of making them think. Perhaps only much later, in the quiet of their own conscience, they may accept the grace to change.

St. Paul at Athens had to be satisfied with incomplete success. He established a point of agreement by saying to the Athenians: "I note that in every respect you are scrupulously religious. As I walked around looking at your shrines, I even discovered an altar inscribed, 'To a God Unknown.' Now, what you are thus worshipping in ignorance I intend to make known to you." At the conclusion of his sermon, most of the Athenians avoided a decision and said, "We will hear you again on this topic some other time," but a few did join Paul and became believers (Ac 17:22 ff.). His success was moderate, but we may guess that without a Point of Agreement he would have lost his audience immediately.

D. Action

These days some preachers are reluctant to tell people directly what they should and should not do. As one priest observed, "If you should all over people, they will should all over you." Paternalism (or maternalism) in preaching to adults is as reprehensible as it is in any adult relationship, and yet there are times when the preacher has the duty of being faithful to a message which demands action, either to accomplish a good or to avoid an evil. When Jesus was asked by a lawyer, "Who is my neighbor?" he could have given an abstract answer: "Everyone is your neighbor." Instead he saw a need for

the General End of Action. He showed what a "neighbor" does
in his illustration which we call the parable of the Good
Samaritan. After telling the story, Jesus challenged his ques-
tioner, "Who was neighbor to the man who fell in with the
robbers?" When the lawyer replied, "The one who treated him
with compassion," Jesus immediately, in accord with the General End of Action, said, "Then go and do the same." (See the
Fifteenth Sunday of the Year C.)

The General End of Action is called for when people
understand a message and appreciate it sufficiently but fail to
act in accord with it. A homily which employs the General End
of Action has three elements: Nature, Motive, and Means. Put
more simply the General End of Action answers the questions,
"What, Why, and How?" The Motives and the Means are major
elements; the Nature is a minor element and usually flows into
the Means if they are properly presented. Although these
elements often determine the organization of a homily, they
are essentially ingredients, and not steps in composition. They
need follow no set order and may intermingle. These three
elements are determined by simple psychology: if you want
people to do something, you must tell them what it is they are
to do (Nature), why they should do it (Motives), and how they
are to go about it (Means).

In the sixth chapter of St. Matthew's gospel, we have an
outline of a sermon with the General End of Action: "Be on
guard against performing religious acts for people to see
(Nature). Otherwise expect no recompense from your heavenly Father (Motive). When you give alms, for example, do not
blow a horn before you in synagogues and streets like hypo-
crites looking for applause (Means). You can be sure of this
much, they are already repaid (back to Motive). In giving alms
you are not to let your left hand know what your right hand is
doing. Keep your deeds of mercy secret (more Means), and
your Father who sees in secret will repay you (Motive)."

Compelling Motives are indispensable for achieving the

General End of Action. They often partake of the qualities which are found in the General End of Impression, especially emotional values. This is not to say that two General Ends are employed. Rather, the qualities of Impression are a means for achieving the End of Action, and are not an end in themselves as is the case with the General End of Impression. An effective homily has one General End. If several motives are employed, especially when several are needed to appeal to a varied audience, they should through a common value add up to a single motive.

Even if you have presented convincing motives for Action, your audience needs to know precisely how to go about doing what you say they should. They need to know the means which will accomplish the end. These means should be specific and concrete. They are both positive (you show them what to do) and negative (you meet their objections). Without specific and concrete Means the homily will result only in platitudes. Notice how specific Jesus is with means (which are mingled with some motives) in this excerpt from the Sermon on the Mount: "You have heard the commandment imposed on our forefathers, 'Do not take a false oath; rather, make good to the Lord all your pledges.' What I tell you is: do not swear at all. Do not swear by heaven (it is God's throne), nor by the earth (it is his footstool), nor by Jerusalem (it is the city of the great King); do not swear by your head (you cannot make a single hair white or black). Say 'Yes' when you mean 'Yes,' and 'No' when you mean 'No.' Anything beyond that is from the evil one" (Mt 5:13 ff.).

It is helpful to see that in the General End of Action, the Statement of Aim expresses the Nature (what) and the Central Idea expresses the Motive (why). In this General End the two can often be joined by the conjunction, "because." For example: Statement of Aim: I want priests in preaching to follow the method of Jesus as recorded in the gospels because (Central Idea) we are called not only to proclaim the message of Jesus but to do so according to his method. "The Little Method" of St. Vincent de Paul is well suited to attain the General End of Action (please see Chapter XVIII for a presentation of St. Vincent's Method).

Remember to stay within one General End in your sermon or homily. There seems to be a particular temptation to change the conclusion into an appeal for action even when action is not the General End. Be convinced that each General End has worth and practical value in itself, especially when the element of personal implication is treated properly within the body of the talk. Each of the four General Ends will be treated further in subsequent chapters.

CHAPTER IX

INTRODUCTIONS AND CONCLUSIONS

"God has made everything appropriate to its time... from beginning to end." (Ec 3:11)

A. Introductions

The time to compose an introduction is when you have completed the body of your homily. You should decide on an introduction only after you have clearly in mind what you want to accomplish through your determination of a General End, a Statement of Aim, and a Central Idea and have allowed these factors to guide your composition. The introduction is important. If it fails, you may lose the audience for the entire homily. Keep in mind these purposes of an introduction: 1) to establish contact with the audience, 2) to arouse interest and attention, and 3) to disclose the message.

Establishing Contact

People want to feel that the preacher is speaking to them, that the homily is a personal matter, a real communication in which a bond is established between preacher and congregation. In order to discover an appropriate bond, think about what may already be in the minds of your audience. There was no doubt what was uppermost in the minds of people in Northern California on the Sunday following the Bay Area earthquake which struck just as a World Series game was about to begin in October of 1989. Nor did anyone have to guess what people were thinking about in a parish in Illinois on the Sunday after a terrible tragedy: two teenagers ended their lives in a murder-suicide pact. In 1991 the Second Sunday of Ordinary Time fell on January 20th, just four days after war began in the Persian Gulf. People sat in church stunned by the tragic events, vainly trying to comprehend their meaning and their magnitude. Any preacher who ignored this state of mind did not make contact with his audience. Every year on the Sunday nearest January 22nd many Catholics remember the decision by the Supreme Court in Roe vs. Wade which in a moment set aside our centuries old Judeo-Christian ethic regarding the sanctity of human life in all its stages. Momentous or striking events are the material of effective Introductions. Not every absorbing event is tragic. On Super Bowl Sunday even people who are not football fans know that a big game will be played that afternoon. It helps to watch the news on TV, to scan the paper, to flip through *Time* or *Newsweek*. Ask yourself, "What is in the minds of my audience?" Of course when the preacher begins with what is uppermost in the minds of his audience, he must relate that event or idea to his message.

Referring to simple realities which are part of our lives can spark interest. William Zinsser in *Life* magazine quite some time ago introduced an essay by writing, "I've often wondered what goes into a hot dog. Now I know and I wish I didn't." I have heard that observation made rather frequently (without credit) because its humor in relation to the common hot dog catches our attention. Actually it is not a bad introduction for a homily on the Twenty Second Sunday of the Year A ("If a man wishes to come after me, he must deny his very self, take up his cross, and begin to follow in my footsteps"). When we learn what goes into being a true disciple of Jesus, we may wish that we did not know.

Arousing Interest and Attention

Some preachers try to use one of the following techniques as part of every introduction: making striking statements ("Jesus is asking the impossible when he demands that we give up everything to follow him"), saying something which demands an explanation ("Jesus seems to be telling us that there is a time when divorce is permitted"), asking questions ("Can any person of faith really believe that God is pleased with abortion?"), employing a paradox ("G.K. Chesterton once said that anything worth doing is worth doing poorly").

Beginning with a question must be done prudently. Some preachers begin with what is actually a silly question: "Have you ever seen a movie you didn't like?" or "Did you ever find it hard to get out of bed in the morning?" The answer to questions of this type is "Of course," and the preacher is no further along than before he started. If you want to begin with a question, make it provocative, something which will make the audience think: "If today the Lord calls us through death to himself, will there be one thing which we will deeply regret not having done?"

Disclosing the Message

Audiences usually want to know at the beginning what your homily will be about. After you have begun your homily they should not be asking themselves questions such as "Where is he going?" or "What is this all about?" or "What in the world is he trying to say?" Do not make it hard for your audience to follow you. Your introduction must flow from your Central Idea and lead the audience to your Statement of Aim. Sometimes you may want to hold off a clear statement of your message to create suspense, but this technique must be used very carefully. At other times you may judge that the audience is hostile to your message and you find it prudent to disclose the message only gradually (this approach is particularly useful when the General End is Persuasion). The principle that you should disclose the message does not mean that you should be trite ("In the gospel Jesus tells us to forgive one another") or banal ("My dear friends, today I shall speak to you about the great commandment of love"). This principle simply means that everything you say in a homily should be guided by your Central Idea.

When you employ your Central Idea, your opening remarks are a true introduction, otherwise they are only a way of getting started. For example on the Seventh Sunday of the Year in the B cycle St. Mark tells the story of how Jesus forgave the sins of the paralytic and cured him of his affliction. Let us say that my General End is Clearness. My Statement of Aim is that I want my audience to understand that in the sacrament of penance the words of Christ absolve us from our sins. My Central Idea is that the words of Christ effect what they say. I could get started with a rather startling story: "A father was driving his twelve year old son to little league. As they were making a left turn, they were hit broadside by a speeding car. The father was uninjured; although his young son miraculously survived, he would never again play little league or any other sport. His neck was broken and he was left paralyzed for life. Today's gospel tells the story of another young man who was paralyzed...." That is a beginning but not an introduction. A less dramatic but true introduction would be: "It has often been said that a picture is worth a thousand words. But one word from Jesus is worth more than a thousand pictures. His word is powerful. It actually makes something happen as we can see from today's gospel."

Think about the introduction to the parable for the Thirtieth-Sunday of the Year C: "Two men went up the temple to pray; one was a Pharisee, the other a tax collector." The audience was made up of those "who believed in their own self-righteousness while holding everyone else in contempt." I can imagine some of them wondering, "Is he finally going to condemn these tax collectors who have no piety?" Others, I think, were more cautious and asked themselves, "What is he up to now? Don't tell us he is going to favor the tax collector." This simple introduction aroused the attention of Jesus' audience.

General Method of Introduction

It is not always possible to come up with a fascinating or provocative introduction. Sometimes you need to use a general method which begins with a statement of a truth with which the audience is familiar and which is related to your Central Idea. You then use a transitional sentence or two to lead to your Central Idea. In speaking about the sacrament of baptism you might say: "In a hospital maternity ward everybody wants to stop and look at the babies in their cribs. We are fascinated with birth and the arrival of a new life into our world. Baptism is for all of us a new birth, the way of receiving God's life as his children. Baptism is a reality which should be fascinating to all of us."

The three purposes of the introduction are not steps to follow. Rather they are ingredients which blend together to make a good introduction. In other words, when you are composing an introduction you should remember that your purpose is to get contact with your audience, to arouse their interest, and to disclose your message. Take the trouble to work out an introduction. Beginning a homily by saying something like, "In today's gospel we see Jesus working a wonderful miracle," gives the impression that the preacher has not prepared properly.

In order to get a good start, it is helpful to memorize your

introduction. The introduction is sufficiently important to
warrant time and attention during the preparation of your
homily. If you do not win the audience and get their attention
at the beginning of your homily, it is not likely that you will do
so later on.

B. The Conclusion

The conclusion of a homily is equally as important as the
introduction. A sound principle is, "When you quit, quit all
over." Your voice and your demeanor, as well as your composition, should let everyone know that you have come to the
end. Never use "stage directions" such as "In conclusion," or
"Finally," or "My last point is." Often preachers ramble on after
they have told the audience that they are about to conclude.
Someone has observed that optimists are those people who
put their shoes back on when the preacher says, "And now in
conclusion."

The purpose of the conclusion is to leave the audience
with your Central Idea. Think how forceful and definite is the
conclusion of the parable on the servant whose huge debt was
wiped out by the king but who failed even to be patient with his
fellow servant who owed him only a small debt: "Then in anger
the master handed him over to the torturers until he paid back
all that he owed. My heavenly Father will treat you in exactly
the same way unless each of you forgives his brother from his
heart" (Twenty-Third Sunday of Year A). During his sermon
on the mount in Matthew's gospel, Jesus called for a deeper
spirituality, a more generous spirit. He concluded that section
by saying succinctly: "In a word, you must become perfect as
your heavenly Father is perfect" (Seventh Sunday of Year A).

In the conclusion stick with your General End. A common mistake is to change from Clearness, Impression, or
Persuasion to Action. The reason for the change seems to be
that some preachers judge that a homily is not practical unless

it tells people what they should do. When Action is brought into the conclusion of a homily which has been guided by one of the other General Ends, there is not sufficient time to develop the elements which lead to Action, especially the treatment of practical means. Some preachers always end with an exhortation to pray ("And so let us pray that we will be forgiving toward those who have offended us and let us ask the Lord to give his grace to those who have enmity toward others"). If the message of the homily leads to petitions, they should be included in the General Intercessions and not presented as a substitute for an appropriate conclusion.

If the preacher has not prepared a definite conclusion, he may find it difficult to find a satisfactory way to stop. Sometimes a preacher is like an airplane pilot who cannot see through the fog and keeps circling the field, searching for a place to land. The fog may be of his own making. A homily which is not organized and unified around a single General End, a definite Statement of Aim, and a clear Central Idea is going to be so foggy that even the preacher does not know how to put it all together in a conclusion. Worse still is when the preacher seems to have landed his plane only to take off again. The author of the book of Ecclesiastes must have experienced such sermons because he wrote, "Better is the end of speech than its beginning" (7:8).

The mortal sin against a good conclusion is to introduce a new idea at the end of your homily. In fact, you should not make any statement which is not definitely related to your development in the body of the homily. If you have worked out a good introduction, you may find that it adds unity to your homily if you refer back to your introduction in your conclusion. ("Whether we continue to eat hot dogs after we know what goes into them does not really matter. What does matter is for us to continue to follow Jesus even after we understand what goes into being a disciple.")

Just as it is helpful to memorize the introduction in order

to get off to a good start, so it is helpful to memorize the conclusion in order to end on a note of finality.

SUMMARY:

The purposes of the Introduction are to establish contact with the audience, to arouse their interest, and to reveal the message. The Conclusion should leave the audience thinking about your Central Idea. Never introduce a new idea in your Conclusion.

EXERCISE:

Write out an Introduction and Conclusion for the material which you have composed for each of the four General Ends from the previous chapter.

PART TWO

FORMS OF PREACHING

"Preaching the gospel is not the subject of a boast; I am under compulsion and have no choice..." (1 Cor 9:16)

"If you live according to my teaching, you are truly my disciples; then you will know the truth, and the truth will set you free."

Jn 8:32

CHAPTER X

DOCTRINAL SERMONS

*"Preach the word ... constantly teaching and
never losing patience." (2 Tm 4:2)*

A Jewish scholar once observed that in a synagogue the chief symbol is the scroll, which signifies knowledge, but in a Christian church the chief symbol is the cross, which signifies suffering. Of course we would hope that through the preaching of the Paschal mystery people would come to see the cross as a sign of glory, and we should also hope that through doctrinal preaching people would come to a proper knowledge of their faith.

Doctrinal preaching is appropriate when people either need to understand something about their faith or when they need to appreciate it. The former calls for the General End of Clearness and the latter for the General End of Impression. Doctrinal preaching may be either homilies within the liturgy or sermons and instructions outside its celebration. In either case it is important to follow the principles for the General Ends of Clearness and Impression (see Chapter VIII).

Doctrinal Homilies from Scripture

A preacher should not approach the liturgical scriptures with pre-conceived ideas. He should allow the scriptures to form within him not only the message but also the manner of preaching it. Sometimes that message is best presented as a doctrinal topic by means of the General End of either Clearness or Impression.

The B cycle features the gospel according to Mark, but since that gospel consists of only sixteen chapters it is supplemented on five Sundays, the Nineteenth through the Twenty-Third, by pericopes from the sixth chapter of St. John. On the Twentieth Sunday of the B cycle we hear Jesus proclaim: "He who feeds on my flesh and drinks my blood has life eternal, and I will raise him up on the last day. For my flesh is real food and my blood is real drink." He then goes on to say, "The one who feeds on my flesh and drinks my blood remains in me, and I in him." It would be appropriate on this Sunday to preach a doctrinal homily on the meaning of the Eucharist, perhaps as follows, General End: Clearness. Statement of Aim: "I want my audience to understand that the Eucharist is the pledge and promise of resurrection. Central Idea: The Eucharist brings us into union with the risen Lord."

The gospel of the Tenth Sunday of Year C presents a beautifully touching scene. It is the story of the widow of Nain. St. Luke tells us that when Jesus realized that this widow was about to bury her only son, he was moved with pity upon seeing her (and I like to believe that he saw in his mind's eye that his own widowed mother one day would follow the lifeless body of her only son to the tomb). He restored the young man to life and gave him back to his mother. It seems to me that on this Sunday one could preach a doctrinal homily with the General End of Impression. Statement of Aim: "I want my audience to appreciate the profundity of Jesus' compassion." Central Idea: "In Jesus we see that God loves us with a human heart."

Doctrinal Homilies from Liturgy

The Constitution on the Liturgy informs us that the homily "draws its content mainly from scriptural and liturgical sources" (no. 35). More specifically the General Instruction of the Roman Missal states: "The homily develops some point of the readings or of another text from the Ordinary or from the Proper of the Mass of the day" (no. 41). The point is that a true homily may flow, not only from the scriptures of the day, but also from some other part of the liturgy. This fact is based on the liturgical axiom, "Lex orandi, lex credendi," — prayer expresses our faith. We might add another liturgical axiom, "Orthopraxis expresses orthodoxy." To realize the full meaning of these axioms, we need to understand that God's revelation is contained in Tradition and Scripture which are not two separate sources, but one expression in two forms. The Dogmatic Constitution on the Church states emphatically: "Sacred tradition and sacred Scripture form one sacred deposit of the word of God which is committed to the Church" (no. 10). Actually we would do well at times to avoid any suggestion of dichotomy regarding scripture and tradition by speaking of scripture and the other teachings of the Church. It is precisely because an important expression of these other teachings is found in the prayers and practices of the liturgy that a true homily may be drawn from liturgical sources. Two obvious examples are the dogmas of the Immaculate Conception and Assumption. Although neither is found explicitly in scripture, both have enjoyed liturgical witness. Homilies on these two Solemnities are rightly drawn from the respective prefaces or presidential prayers assigned to these days. Even when a doctrine is found in scripture, it may be helpful to preach from liturgical sources; for example, on the Solemnity of Corpus Christi a true homily could be developed on the holy Eucharist from one of the eight elements of the eucharistic prayer or from one or other of the Prefaces of the Holy Eucharist.

Before the liturgical reforms of the Second Vatican Council, some priests preached at Mass on topics which they had chosen, or which a chancery office had assigned, with no consideration for the scriptures of the day. Now at the other

extreme some purists seem to think that nothing except the
scriptures of the day may be preached, and they appear to be
unaware that liturgical sources are appropriate. By following
the principles of the Council and the directives of the General
Instruction of the Roman Missal, the fullness of our faith may
be proclaimed not only within the liturgical celebration of the
Eucharist but as truly part of it.

When Further Instruction Is Needed

Almost a century ago Pope Pius X in his encyclical *Acerbo
Nimis* decreed that catechesis must be provided on occasions
outside of Mass and must not substitute for a Sunday sermon.
The objection to his point then was, and at times still is, that
Sunday is simply the best time to reach the majority of parishioners. It is true that no matter how many instruction classes
you offer in a parish, you will reach only a small number of
people. That is why some bishops and priests insist that on
Sunday people need more teaching than the scriptures and
the liturgy can provide, and they adhere to the notion that a
syllabus of topics and outlines should be organized for Sunday
preaching.

Leaving aside the arguments in favor of and against a
syllabus, all concerned should recognize two facts. The first is
that the law of the Church requires that a homily be given at
Mass on Sundays. Canon 767 declares: "Whenever a congregation is present a homily is to be given at all Sunday Masses and
at Masses celebrated on holy days of obligation." This same
canon defines what it means by a homily: "In a homily the
mysteries of faith and the norms of Christian living are to be
expounded from the sacred text throughout the course of the
liturgical year." We have just seen that the "sacred text" includes both scripture and liturgical prayers. The law, it must be
admitted, is not iron-clad: it says that the homily "cannot be
omitted without a serious reason." The law does not suggest

what a serious reason might be, but it should be noted that the Latin text is stronger than the translation "serious reason." The Latin is *gravi de causa*. When we appreciate that a true homily is an integral part of liturgy, I think we conclude that we must not omit it or substitute something for it any more than we would omit the gospel or substitute some reading for it.

A Helpful Compromise

To omit a true homily in favor of a syllabus of assigned topics is not in accord with the law, not to mention the meaning of a liturgical celebration, but a second fact must be recognized which leads to a helpful compromise. When a priest keeps his homily within a reasonable time limit, it is possible, even desirable, to give an instruction following the Prayer after Communion when announcements may be made. In some places a series of instructions was given at this time of the Mass when the practice of taking Holy Communion in the hand was restored and when the new Rite of the Sacrament of Penance was introduced. It is an ideal time for teaching, but the presentation must be within a time limit of no more than five minutes. Much can be said in a well organized presentation, even if it is brief. The priest need not give this instruction himself; any qualified person may do so. I must admit that those who leave early will miss the instruction, but we simply cannot reach everyone. This compromise, although not perfect, meets the requirement of law regarding a homily and the need for instruction. Examples of topics for instruction are the Church's teaching on abortion, war, economics, social justice, and sexual morality.

Other types of presentations should not replace a homily. Missionary appeals, vocation talks, financial reports, and the like should be given after Holy Communion before the dismissal. The presider and the presenter must cooperate with each other and agree to share the time available at Mass. The effort necessary for achieving this cooperation is preferable to substituting a talk in place of a homily. Not only can this be done; it has been done with success. Occasionally it is possible to integrate a special topic into a true homily, but an artificial connection should be avoided in favor of presenting the special topic after communion.

All of this is not to say that a preacher may not be helped by a syllabus of topics and a set of outlines which are drawn from scripture and other liturgical sources and which can be developed into true homilies. The point is that whatever is done must be in accord with both the law which guides the liturgy and the spirit which informs it. The liturgical homily is too important to be replaced since the liturgy, of which the homily is an integral part, is the indispensable source of the true Christian spirit.

SUMMARY:

Doctrinal preaching is appropriate when people either need to understand something about their faith or when they need to appreciate something about it. The General End of doctrinal sermons is either clearness or impression. Sometimes the liturgy calls for a doctrinal homily.

EXERCISE:

Compose a sermon on one of the following or a similar topic: Why the Church baptizes infants, the position of the Church on abortion, why the Church calls for full, active participation in the liturgy, the place of music in the liturgy, the meaning of the Assumption.

CHAPTER XI

BIBLICAL PREACHING

*"All scripture is inspired by God and is useful
for teaching, reproof, correction, and
training in holiness." (2 Tm 3:16)*

The importance of biblical preaching is based on a truth which was enunciated by the Second Vatican Council in its *Dogmatic Constitution on Divine Revelation (Dei Verbum,* no. 21): "The Church has always venerated the divine Scriptures just as she venerates the body of the Lord, since from the table of both the word of God and the body of Christ she unceasingly receives and offers to the faithful the bread of life, especially in the sacred liturgy."

Cardinal Ratzinger observed in his commentary on *Dei Verbum* that some of the fathers of the council objected to this statement in the draft document because they thought it detracted from the veneration due to the Blessed Sacrament, but when it came to a vote the statement stood because it expresses the sound and consistent teaching of the Church, even though in practice we may not always have been influenced properly by it. The *Constitution on the Sacred Liturgy,* promulgated as the first document of the Council, had already declared that "Christ is present in his word, since it is he himself who speaks when the holy scriptures are read in the church" (no. 7). So sacred are the scriptures that they must be constantly proclaimed by the Church through her preachers. We should no more neglect the scriptures than we would the Blessed Sacrament. The priest who is the minister of the sacrament is the preacher of the word. Biblical preaching is integral to his vocation.

The Nature of Biblical Preaching

Biblical preaching is based on the truth that God is consistent. You can depend on God. What God has done, that is what he will do. What God has said, that is what he will say. God freed his people from the slavery of Egypt; then he would surely free his people from slavery in Babylon. There was an exodus from Egypt; then there would be a new exodus from Babylon. Further, that which happened to the people of the Old Covenant happens in its own way to the people of the New Covenant. This biblical doctrine of consistency is the basis for the Preface of Thanksgiving day for the dioceses of the United States and is reflected in these few lines: "Father... once you chose a people and gave them a destiny and, when you brought them out of bondage to freedom, they carried with them the promise that all people would be blessed and all people could be free." The only surprise in God's consistency is that he opens his heart more widely to his people as we progress through the fullness of time to the Day of the Lord. Like Father, like Son. That is why the Letter to Hebrews says that "Jesus Christ is the same yesterday, today, and forever" (13:8).

Scripture is not the words of men only; it is the word of God. It has an inherent value, a preciousness, which God wishes all his people to profit from. It has a greater value than any merely human word. Scripture is also practical. It is not entertainment or diversion. Although it may be approached as literature, it is much more than that. It is the Lord himself who speaks to us, and the Lord means his word to be effective so that it does not return to him void. Sound biblical preaching is God's instrument for making his word effective. This preaching is not taking a quotation from scripture as a jumping off point for a sermon, nor is it the presentation of several texts to support the preacher's idea. It does not even begin with the people and their needs. It begins with the bible itself. It goes to the bible for the source of the sermon. Its purpose is to communicate to the audience the message of a biblical passage. It is not merely exegesis or history. It attempts to make people contemporaneous with God's initial communication, and to make God's communication contemporaneous with people today. Biblical preaching is based on the conviction that God's word is always what people need to hear because God's word is perennial.

This chapter is concerned primarily with the Hebrew scriptures, the Old Testament. They are of value to us because "all scripture is inspired by God," and because the God of Israel is the God of Christians. There are not two Gods, the one of the Old Testament who is a God of wrath and vengeance and the God of the New who is a God of mercy and compassion. A bleak, forbidding picture of God which some people seem to draw from the Old Testament is simply a false portrait. God was, is, and always will be the loving God revealed to us in Jesus Christ. The only change is not in God but in our understanding of him, an understanding which is never complete, not even in the beatific vision of heaven.

There is absolutely no potency in God, no potential. God is pure act. God is not becoming. God is. He is a complete book. We, the entire people of God from "the days of Abraham and Moses" through this moment of the Church, are reading God's book of himself. We are getting through it. Each generation of faith receives the grace to remember what we as a people have already pondered while we continue to read on. The wonder and the majesty of God is such that we will never complete the book. That is one reason why we will not be bored with the eternity of heaven. We will never exhaust the beauty and goodness of God, we will never finish God as we do some course in school so that we end up sitting around wondering what to do next. This reality of God is beautifully expressed in the Alternate Opening Prayer on the Second Sunday of Lent: "Father of light, in you is found no shadow of change but only the fullness of life and limitless truth."

The office of preaching is to proclaim the story of God, not as something relegated to the past but as an expression, however feeble, of God's eternal "now." As John Shea explains in his book, *Stories of God*, "Although these (biblical) stories begin with 'long ago,' they end up with 'right now.'" To put it another way, God's story begins "Once upon a time," but it moves to "This is the acceptable time! This is the day of salvation!" (2 Cor. 6:2). The contemporary expression of God's consistent love is the reason why people living long after the return from the Babylonian captivity can pray Psalm 126: "When the Lord delivered Zion from bondage / it seemed like a dream. / Then was *our* mouth filled with laughter,/ on *our* lips there were songs. / The heathens themselves said: 'What marvels the Lord worked for them!' What marvels the Lord worked for us! / Indeed *we* were glad."

Deuteronomic Preaching

Biblical preaching is exemplified in the Book of Deuteronomy, the fifth book of the Old Testament. Its form is different from the previous four books. It consists mainly of sermons on the Book of Exodus which were composed centuries after the events which it treats. The preacher speaks in the person of Moses. The purpose of his presentation is to proclaim again the ancient tradition in time of great crisis for Israel. Its message is not in the past tense, "Thus said the Lord God," but in the present tense, "Thus says the Lord God."

Consider the great profession of faith in Deuteronomy 26:5-6 which was to be proclaimed within a liturgical celebration; note its subtle change from the third person to the first person: "A wandering Aramean was my father who went down to Egypt with a small household and lived there as an alien. But there he became a nation great, strong and numerous (note the third person). When the Egyptians maltreated and oppressed us, (now the change to the first person, to the people living centuries after the event) imposing hard labor on us, we cried to the Lord, the God of our fathers, and he heard our cry and saw our affliction, our toil and our oppression. He brought us out of Egypt with his strong hand and outstretched arm, with terrifying power, with signs and wonders; and bringing us into this country, he gave us this land flowing with milk and honey."

The preacher of Deuteronomy even goes so far as to deny rhetorically an aspect of the former event in order to emphasize God's current action, an action which is in accord with his past way of dealing with his people: "Hear, O Israel, the statutes and decrees which I proclaim in your hearing this day, that you may learn them and take care to observe them. The LORD, our God, made a covenant with us at Horeb; not with our fathers did he make this covenant [this denial is the rhetorical device] but with us [this is his point], all of us who are alive here this day" (5:1:3).

An understanding of the Deuteronomic literature helps us to understand the shallowness of the error of seeing God as in process and leads us to the proper approach to biblical preaching, which is based on the consistency of God.

Exegesis and Hermeneutic

Biblical preaching relies on sound exegesis. It recognizes that the preacher must penetrate the medium to find the message (see Chapter IV). All the tools of exegesis help, especially historical, literary, and form criticism, as well as the analogy of faith (this latter being understood as the principle

of comparing one aspect of faith with another). The preacher
should learn to consult sound commentaries, such as *The New
Jerome Biblical Commentary* and *The Collegeville Bible Commentary*,
and other homiletic helps which supply exegesis, such as
Fuller's *Preaching the Lectionary*. But exegesis is not preaching.
It is a preparation for preaching. The sermon or homily
should contain only such exegesis as is necessary for the
audience to see the message clearly and to be satisfied that the
preacher is presenting an authentic message.

The heart of biblical preaching is the homiletic
hermeneutic. This homiletic hermeneutic is a movement
from what God has said to what God says, from what God has
done to what God does. It is putting the message into a
medium from which the audience can create a meaning for
themselves which is in accord with God's message. Determining and composing the homiletic hermeneutic is often more
difficult than the work of exegesis. Sometimes all of our prayer
and reflection begets nothing. We need help from someone
else who has done the work before us. And yet we hear the stern
warning, "Do not use canned homilies." Of course we should
not memorize someone else's homily, or even worse read it
verbatim to the people, but we can and often should consult
books of homilies, whether contemporary, classical, or patristic
to search for a starter, for a spark of imagination to get us
going, or a stimulus to our own thinking. After all, how creative
can we be Sunday after Sunday and day after day? There is a
proper way to use the exegetical material of scholars and there
is a proper way to use the homiletic material of practiced
preachers.

Some Examples

Now to some examples. We hear the beginning of the
Book of Genesis at Mass on Monday of the Fifth Week of the
Year I. The following brief homily is mostly exegesis, however

simple, but it moves in the final paragraph to a homiletic hermeneutic:

> "Although today is the middle of the month, we mark a beginning. We have heard the beginning of the Book of Genesis which tells the story of the beginning of creation. It is a beautifully poetic account. The purpose of the inspired author was not to present a scientific explanation of the origin of the world. His was a religious purpose. No one should attempt to reconcile the story of Genesis with theories of science, such as evolution, because there simply is no point of comparison. Science attempts to unravel the facts of how the world came to be. Genesis presents the meaning of creation. It does so in a picturesque fashion, suited to the mentality of a people far removed from us in time and culture.
>
> "The Israelites were surrounded by pagan people who believed in many and varied gods. They worshipped the sun, or the moon and the stars, or other created entities as divine. The Israelites were called to worship the one, true God, a personal God of intelligence and love. God was to be worshipped, not his creation, for he was the one who made the sun, the moon and the stars, the plants and all living things. Good things should not replace the cause of goodness, God himself.
>
> "Scientific language can be cold and lifeless. The poetry of the Book of Genesis is meant to be inspiring and uplifting. It should raise our minds and hearts to God the creator. He is a God who is all powerful and who has given us this magnificent world with its many gifts. From what we see all around us we find one of the reasons why the liturgy prays, "Father, all powerful and ever living God, we do well always and everywhere to give you thanks."

At Mass on the Friday after Ash Wednesday we hear a reading from Isaiah 58:1-9 which says in part: "Is this the kind of fasting I wish... that a man bow his head like a reed and lie in sackcloth and ashes? This rather is the fasting I wish: releasing those bound unjustly, untying the thongs of the yoke, setting free the oppressed, breaking every yoke, sharing your bread with the hungry, sheltering the oppressed and the homeless, clothing the naked when you see them, and not turning your back on your own." This declaration is more than a corrective for mistaken notions of piety; it is a homiletic hermeneutic which puts the message into a medium which the people of that time needed. To discover a current hermeneutic, the preacher asks himself, "What does this message say to people today?"

An example from the Mass for Friday of the Twelfth Week of Year II illustrates how an Old Testament exegesis leads to a New Testament hermeneutic. The Old Testament pericope is 2 Kings 25:1-12 and the gospel tells how Jesus cured a leper (Mt 8:1-4):

> "In the year 597 the city of Jerusalem surren-
> dered to the Babylonians. About ten years later
> Zedekiah, a mere puppet king, foolishly rebelled against
> the Babylonians and a second siege followed. The
> temple and much of the city were destroyed and
> people were deported to Babylon. The devastation was
> something which Judah had brought on itself because
> of its blatant infidelity to God. According to its cov-
> enant with God, Judah was to be dedicated to the one
> true God. Without the practice of religion, Judah had
> lost its meaning. It was like a river without water, an
> orchard without trees, a marriage without love.
>
> "And yet all was not lost. Subsequent prophets
> would preach a message of hope. They would call for
> a return to the Lord through a real repentance. Re-
> pentance was still possible because God had not aban-

doned his people. Hope for the future was fulfilled in the person of Jesus Christ. He was the great healer, as we saw in today's gospel. The leper was an outcast, like the people who had been deported to Babylon. The cure of the leper was a sign that Jesus had come to heal the world of the wounds of sin. His form of healing was to reconcile us with God. Sin wounds, but reconciliation heals. Sin separates, but reconciliation unites. In the words of absolution in the sacrament of penance we hear these words: 'God the Father of Mercies through the death and resurrection of his Son has reconciled the world to himself.' We, the people of God, are the beneficiaries of this marvelous reconciliation."

Perspective on Biblical Preaching

Biblical preaching must be authentic; it must not be merely words about God but the word of God itself. Christ speaks when the scriptures are read in the church. The challenge to preachers of the scriptures is, "Does Christ speak through us when we preach?" Further consideration will be given to biblical preaching in the following chapters.

SUMMARY:

This form of preaching begins with the bible itself. It does not consist in taking quotations from scripture as a jumping off point for a sermon; rather, it is concerned with the message of a scriptural pericope.

EXERCISE:

Select any Sunday of Ordinary Time and compose a biblical sermon on the Old Testament pericope.

"The purpose of the sacraments is to sanctify God's people, to build up the Body of Christ, and to give worship to God."

Constitution on the Sacred Liturgy, no. 59

CHAPTER XII

SACRAMENTAL HOMILIES

"My word shall not return to me void, but
shall do my will, achieving the end for
which I sent it." (Is 55:11)

The sacraments are the life of the Church. From them
flows the grace of Christ. According to liturgical principles
every sacrament is to be celebrated with a liturgy of the word,
which includes preaching. I find it difficult to treat preaching
as an integral part of sacraments without a proper context
which includes some consideration of the specific relationship
of the priest to the sacraments. The priest is the sacramental
person of the Church. The sacraments are his life. They are
what he is about since he is the chief instrument of Christ in his
sacraments. Conformity to Christ begins for all Catholics with
the sacraments of Christian initiation. The priest is further
consecrated by the sacrament of ordination. His general
vocation in the Church comes from baptism-confirmation,
but his specific call is from ordination. Ordination is also the
source of his special grace of holiness.

Priestly holiness is sacramental. It is sacramental in this
way. Pope Leo the Great wrote that since the death and
resurrection of Jesus, his power and his love have passed into
the sacraments. Pope Leo added that Christ is more present to
us in his divinity through the sacraments than he was to the

people of his day through his humanity. It would have been wonderful to have lived with Jesus, to have seen his face, to have heard his voice, to have felt his touch. But Jesus was limited in time and space during his life on this earth. He could contact only a relatively few people. He never journeyed to Rome as did Peter, or to Athens as did Paul. In fact, he did not go beyond the confines of Galilee and Judea. But now Jesus has made himself available everywhere to everyone down through the centuries by means of the sacraments. That is why we can say that Jesus is more present to us now in his divinity through the sacraments than he was to the people of his day through his humanity. The sacraments are the humanity of Christ in a kind of extension of the hypostatic union.

We must remember, however, that the sacraments are not things. We do not keep a supply of sacraments locked up somewhere and take them out when we need them, the way in which we might select a can of food from a supermarket shelf or purchase a bottle of medicine at a drug store. The sacraments are transcendent human experiences. They are transcendent in that they bring us into contact with divine power and love. They are human in that they are incarnational, like Christ himself; they are divinity present in and communicated through humanity.

Becoming the Humanity of Christ

Even though all the sacraments are liturgical, there has been an unfortunate tendency to limit the word "liturgy" to the celebration of the Eucharist ("What time is liturgy?" people ask, meaning "What time is the Eucharist?"). Priests must remember that all the sacraments are part of the liturgy of the Church in which they are the humanity of Christ. Christ's divine power and love are communicated to the people now through priests as they were to the people of his day through his humanity. Think for a moment about the significance of the words of absolution in the sacrament of penance: "God, the Father of mercies, through the death and resurrection of his Son, has reconciled the world to himself and sent the Holy Spirit among us for the forgiveness of our sins." There is a cosmic ring to those words. They seem to speak of a worldwide, almost timeless effect: "God has reconciled the world to himself." Next we say, "Through the ministry of the Church may God give you pardon and peace." That is the way in which the sacramental act of forgiveness is channeled to people: through the ministry of the Church. We have narrowed down this cosmic act of God. The Church, however, is not some vague or nebulous force in the world. That is why there is a third sentence to the formula of absolution: "And I absolve you from your sins." Now we have become specific. Who is this "I" who absolves? We know full well that it is not the human person of the priest. When Jesus proclaimed the great "I AM's" of John's gospel, it was the person of the Son of God who spoke. And it is that person who speaks through priests in the sacraments. Priests are the voice and the hand of Christ in a kind of new hypostatic union: they are his humanity in the sacraments.

Sacraments are Liturgical Actions of Christ

Think of the "Great I" of the sacraments: I baptize you, I confirm you. I absolve you. I anoint you. And most of all think of the first person singular in the Eucharist: "Take and eat it. This is MY Body. Take and drink: this is MY blood." People of faith acknowledge that this is now the body and the blood of Christ, not the body and the blood of the priest. We who are priests must ask ourselves whether we fully appreciate what happens through us in the eucharistic prayer, and how closely we are united with Christ at that time and during all the sacraments? The celebration of all the sacraments ought to be our moments of greatest holiness since they are the moments of our greatest union with Christ.

I know a priest who says that he senses a deeper oneness with Christ when he proclaims the sacramental words, "This is my Body, this is my blood," than he does when he actually receives the body and the blood of the Lord. It is something he feels at times, and he is grateful when he does. He says that he then knows what true holiness is. Holiness is not the feeling; it is the reality of which the feeling is a manifestation. Holiness is oneness with Christ.

Perspective on Private and Liturgical Prayer

To grow in oneness with Christ we priests need personal prayer as does everyone else, but we must recognize that celebrating the liturgy with the people is the most profound form of prayer because it is the prayer of Christ the High Priest with whom we are united. We must foster devotion to the real presence of Christ in the Blessed Sacrament and relish those restful moments alone with the Lord. Such devotion ought to beget in us a great desire and enthusiasm for the celebration of the Eucharist with the people. Above all we must fulfill the purpose for which Christ left us the sacramental memorial of his death and resurrection. We cannot afford to neglect meditation and a contemplative spirit, but the liturgy is the summit toward which this activity is to be directed.

Priests more than anyone else must have a "Church" spirituality. That spirituality is drawn from the liturgy, which for everyone is the indispensable source of the true Christian spirit, and which contains for the priest his specific source of sanctity. It is the font from which his holiness flows. Because of individualistic forms of piety and self-centered expressions of prayer, it is possible that the celebration of the sacraments becomes for us a perfunctory performance rather than an act of piety. It is even possible that the celebration of the holy

Eucharist with and for the people seems like a job to be done rather than the highest expression of our identity and the supreme source of holiness as priests. The divine office for many of us is the prayer of an individual rather than the prayer of the Church, and devotion is found alone and in private. During the debate over the *Constitution on the Sacred Liturgy,* one prelate objected to the fundamental principle of the Constitution by declaring, *"Participatio non est nisi distractio"* ("participation is nothing more than a distraction"). That attitude has not been entirely replaced by sound, liturgical piety. While we need a personal, individual relationship with Christ, we as priests are betrayed by schools of spirituality which neglect the liturgy as the primary, essential, and perennial means to grow in holiness.

A priest who over a weekend has two weddings, hears confessions, meets with a number of people in the rectory, celebrates two or three Masses on Sunday, has baptisms in the afternoon, and dutifully prays the Liturgy of the Hours, may feel guilty because he spends late Sunday afternoon and evening reading the paper and watching TV or having dinner with friends rather than "praying." The reason he may feel guilty is that he has been schooled in a spirituality which fits a hermit and not a priest. It is a tragic waste to fail to see how prayerful and spiritual could have been the celebration of all these forms of liturgy. I have often found that devoted priests do not need more opportunities for retreats or private prayer. They need more time for rest and relaxation, provided, of course, that they have participated in the liturgy as the highest form of prayer.

A priest who had been ordained a little more than a year remarked to me that he had been interested in liturgy while he was a seminarian. As a priest he discovered that liturgy is his life. With that perspective we should see that we are not too busy to become holy. What we are busy about is the means to priestly holiness. This is not to advocate the principle that my work is my prayer; rather, it is to acknowledge that prayer is my work. Prayer with and for the people is my work as a priest, my way of living in union with Christ. A priest cannot preach the scriptures unless they have become part of his life, and a priest cannot preach sacramental homilies unless he is imbued with a deep faith in their significance as liturgy. A priest must live and preach according to the doctrine of the Second Vatican Council that "Every liturgical celebration, because it is an action of Christ the priest and of his Body the Church, is a sacred action surpassing all others; no other action of the Church can match its claim to efficacy, nor equal the degree of it" (*Constitution on the Sacred Liturgy,* no. 7). Sacramental homilies must be the expression of solid priestly holiness.

Purpose of Sacramental Homilies

The celebration of the sacraments is not a time for instruction; that is to take place before people approach the sacraments. The purpose of sacramental homilies is to draw people into full, conscious, and active participation in the sacrament which is being celebrated. Although sacraments are effective *ex opere operato,* the full, conscious, and active participation of the people comes about largely *ex opere operantis sacerdotis.* What we do as priests in the manner in which we celebrate the sacraments, including the homily, either enlightens the faith and increases the devotion of the participants or casts a dark and chilling cloud over them.

We must be careful not to lose the concept that all the sacraments are liturgy. As liturgical, the sacraments have a threefold character: 1) they express some truth about God since they are acts of worship, 2) they involve the community which is the Church, and 3) they flow from and lead to the Eucharist. Sacramental homilies are an integral part of sacraments precisely as they are liturgical.

Acts of Worship

Since all the sacraments are liturgy, we should be aware that they are in the first place acts of worship. They acknowledge and express some truth about God. The sacraments of Christian initiation acknowledge that God is a loving Father who brings us into his divine family which on this earth is found in the Church. Through Christian initiation we become conformed to the image of God's Son as the first born of many brothers and sisters. The celebration of baptism-confirmation and first Eucharist praises God as Father and acknowledge that "all life and all holiness" come from him. The sacrament of holy orders acknowledges God as Redeemer and Reconciler through his Son and Servant, Jesus; it is a conformity to Christ as prophet, king, and priest. These are the sacraments of identity in the Church, and so they may never be repeated. As we say, they imprint a permanent character: baptism/confirmation mark us as the People of God and holy orders ordains those who are called to serve God's people.

The sacrament of marriage acknowledges that God is a God of love and praises him as the source of true love. The sacrament of penance acknowledges that God is the Father of mercies and praises him for his limitless forgiveness. Anointing acknowledges that God is the divine healer, and praises him as the one who restores us to full health, eventually in the resurrection.

The Community of the Church

Because they are liturgical, sacramental acts are never private and individual. They involve the Church; they are ecclesial. Baptism/confirmation and first Eucharist are called sacraments of Christian initiation because they "initiate" us into the Church. They are, as the ancient fathers liked to say, the door of the Church. To use another figure, the baptismal font is the womb from which we are born into the family of the Church and in confirmation we are confirmed and verified as family members. Holy Orders is the sacrament of special service in the Church. Priests are ordained not for themselves but for others. This sacrament conforms priests to Christ "who came not to be served, but to serve and to give his life as a ransom for the many."

Marriage is more than the union of individuals; it is a sign of the union of Christ and his Church. It is also the sacrament which brings new members to the womb of the Church. Penance through the ministry of the Church gives pardon and peace and reconciles us to God and one another. Anointing strengthens us to turn from ourselves in the weakness of sickness to remember and be concerned about others.

To and From the Eucharist

"The liturgy is the summit toward which the activity of the Church is directed, as well as the font from which all her power flows" (*Constitution on the Liturgy,* no. 10). What is true of all liturgy is true of the Eucharist in an eminent way. The Eucharist is the summit toward which all the Church's activity, including the other six sacraments, is directed. The Eucharist is also the font from which all the Church's power, including that of the other six sacraments, flows. "The eucharistic action is the very heartbeat of the congregation of the faithful" (*Decree on Ministry and Life of Priests,* no. 5). The Eucharist is central because it is the celebration of the paschal mystery, the death and resurrection of Jesus.

Baptism and its completion in confirmation leads to the Eucharist since the goal is "that all who are made children of God by faith and baptism should come together to praise God in the midst of his Church, to take part in her sacrifice, and to eat the Lord's supper (*Constitution on the Liturgy,* no. 10). The baptized share in the royal priesthood of Christ which is primarily expressed in the liturgy of the Eucharist. Priesthood is so directed toward the Eucharist that without this sacrament a priest is like a composer without a composition or a director without an orchestra.

The sacramental union of Christian marriage finds its highest expression in the union of Christ and his people which is the culmination of the eucharistic sacrifice. Anointing will have its full effect of healing only through the Eucharist as the sacrament of resurrection. Penance is a sacrament for reconciliation and clears the way to full, active participation in the Eucharist which is the sacrament of reconciliation.

All the sacraments may be celebrated within the celebration of the Eucharist after the liturgy of the word, except penance. It is not allowed "to hear confessions" during Mass since two liturgical celebrations are not permitted in the same place at the same time, nor may the Mass be interrupted for the celebration of penance since the Mass is not penitential by its nature.

Sacramental homilies are primarily concerned with proclaiming that through the sacramental action God's word does not return to him void but does his will, achieving the end for which he sends it. The word of Christ, "I baptize you, I confirm you, this is my body, this is my blood, I do, I absolve you, through this anointing may the Lord... help you... and raise you up," all these instances of the word of Christ are effective in the sacramental action. In fact, in the sacraments word and action combine to form one reality. It is this reality which sacramental homilies are to proclaim.

SUMMARY:

The purpose of sacramental homilies is not to instruct people but to lead them into full, conscious, and active participation in the celebration of the sacraments when they are experiencing them.

EXERCISE:

Compose a brief homily for a baptism, for a wedding, and for a funeral.

CHAPTER XIII

PREPARING FOR SUNDAY

*"Today is holy to the Lord your God.
Do not be sad and do not weep for
today is holy to our Lord.
Do not be saddened this day, for rejoicing in
the Lord must be your strength."
(Ne 8:9-10)*

"On the Lord's Day Christ's faithful should come together into one place so that, by hearing the word of God and
taking part in the Eucharist, they may call to mind the passion,
the resurrection, and the glorification of the Lord Jesus, and
may thank God who 'has begotten us again through the
resurrection of Jesus Christ from the dead unto a living hope.'
Hence the Lord's day is the original feast day" (*Constitution on
the Sacred Liturgy*, no. 106).

The principal ministry of a priest is fulfilled in the
celebration of the Sunday Eucharist. He is responsible for a
comprehensive preparation of the Eucharist which leads the
people to that conscious, full, active participation in the liturgy
which is the indispensable source of the true Christian spirit.
Ideally he carries out this preparation in collaboration with a
liturgy committee, but as the presider he bears the ultimate
responsibility for a complete and cohesive plan. Since the
homily is an integral part of the liturgy, it should not be

132 ORDAINED TO PREACH

composed as if it were an event in isolation from the rest of the liturgy. Actually preparation for the homily should begin only after all the elements of the celebration have been considered.

Theme

After prayer and study, the first step is to determine a theme. Liturgists are generally opposed to "thematic liturgies," which manipulate or change texts to create a topic. Determining a theme, in contrast, is sifting from the richness of mystery a specific aspect of truth. The goal is not to impose a pre-conceived idea but to draw a theme from the liturgy of the day. Actually the theme of every eucharistic celebration is the paschal mystery, the death and resurrection of Christ, and yet the paschal mystery is such a rich truth that within it and flowing from it are specific expressions. It is one of these specifics which forms the theme of a particular celebration, especially as that specific relates to the needs of the people at the time.

On Ordinary Sundays of the Year you usually begin by studying the gospel in the light of the liturgical observance. For example, in the C cycle the parable of the Prodigal Son is read both on the Fourth Sunday of Lent as well as on the Twenty-Fourth Sunday of the Year. Within Lent you may sense a message which is somewhat different from the message on the Ordinary Sunday of the Year, even though the gospel is the same. Looking at the first reading may also influence your interpretation of the gospel, as may also the prayers assigned to the day. Any message must be judged by the needs of the people. Will they be able to derive a suitable and helpful meaning for themselves from this message? When you have settled on the message, you are ready to formulate the theme, preferably in one short sentence.

"After greeting the people the priest, deacon, or other suitable minister may very briefly introduce the Mass of the day" (*General Instruction of the Roman Missal*, no. 29). This introduction is the statement of the theme, which could be something like this: "Through our baptism Christ has called us to the dignity of a royal priesthood." The statement of the theme is not a mini-homily. Remember that it should be expressed in one sentence, perhaps two. Another example: "Today we are challenged by Christ to put him first in our lives."

Introduction to the Readings

The purpose of an introduction to the readings is to help the people to listen to and to hear the scriptural pericopes intelligently. It is a mistake to think that every selection requires an introduction or that for some reason we must follow a consistent method. If the readings require no introduction, do not make one up. An introduction is not a summary, nor is it a brief homily. Take the first reading of the Twenty-Eighth Sunday of the Year, Cycle C. It tells the story of Naaman the Syrian who was cured of leprosy by bathing in the Jordan river (2 K 5:14-17). As the people sit to listen, they hear the reading begin in this way: "Naaman went down and plunged into the Jordan seven times at the word of Elisha." The pericope takes up in the middle of the story, and most people have no idea of the context. An introduction is needed.

The following is a summary and not an introduction: "In today's first reading, Naaman, a Syrian, was a leper. When he followed the directions given him by Elisha, the prophet, he went and bathed seven times in the Jordan river and was cured. Then he wanted to express his thanks." All of that is what the reading says. Let the reading speak for itself.

The following is homiletic, as well as too lengthy, and not introductory: "Naaman was a leper who at first hesitated to follow the directions given him by the prophet, Elisha. He thought that to bathe in the Jordan river was too simple, too

ordinary, since he could have bathed in one of the rivers back
home. He discovered, however, that the power of God came
upon him when he humbled himself to wash his sores in the
Jordan river. He shows us the kind of humble faith we are to
have." Use these ideas in the homily where they belong.

An introduction should be brief and say only what the
people need to hear so that they may follow the reading. The
reading from the Book of Kings could be introduced in this
way:

"The background of the Old Testament reading is that a
man named Naaman came to Israel from Damascus in Syria in
search of a cure for his leprosy." This one sentence is sufficient.
It lets the people know that the story is from the Old Testament, not the New, and prepares them to make sense of the
reading as they hear it.

The nature of the introduction is determined by the
literary form of the scriptural reading. These forms are A)
narration (as in most of the gospels and the Old Testament
stories), B) proclamation (the words of the prophets and the
sermons in the Acts of the Apostles), C) exposition (the
epistles and the wisdom literature), and D) prayers (this last is
rarely found in liturgical pericopes; an example is the first
reading for the Sixteenth Sunday of the Year, Cycle A). Each
literary form calls for a distinct type of introduction.

A) *Narration.* The pericope will rarely present a story
which is complete in itself. Sometimes it is necessary to give the
context, especially if the story is from the Old Testament. The
first reading for the Twenty-Ninth Sunday of the Year in the C
cycle is from the Book of Exodus. It tells the story of how Moses
kept his hands raised in prayer with the support of Aaron and
Hur for the success of the Israelites against the Amalekites.
Introduction: "After the Israelites had been freed from slavery
in Egypt and while they were wandering in the desert, they
encountered a hostile tribe led by a man called Amalek."

B. *Proclamation.* On the 15th Sunday of the Year A we read
from the fifty-fifth chapter of the prophet Isaiah. A simple,
brief introduction is sufficient: "The prophet speaks in the
voice of God about the value of his word, the revelation of his
mercy." This introduction helps the listeners to know immediately that God is speaking through the prophet and that the
phrase "my word" means God's revelation. The context is
indicated, which is a treatment of God's mercy. There is no
need to go into the matter of authorship or to use a technical
term such as "Deutero-Isaiah." Regarding the sermons from
the Acts of the Apostles, which are presented on the Sundays
of the Easter season, it is helpful to indicate their setting. For
example, on the Third Sunday of Easter, Cycle A: "Our first
reading is taken from a sermon which St. Peter preached to a
large crowd on Pentecost Sunday."

C. *Exposition.* An explanation of the background makes
for a helpful introduction to most pericopes from the epistles
of the New Testament and the Wisdom Literature of the Old
Testament. The second reading for the 14th Sunday of the
Year A is from parts of the eighth chapter of Romans, which
could be introduced by saying, "In the following section of his
letter to the Romans St. Paul speaks of the consequences of the
sacrament of baptism." On the other hand, the pericope for
the following Sunday from the same chapter requires no
introduction. From the Wisdom Literature the Sunday Readings present selections from Proverbs, Ecclesiastes, Sirach,
and the Book of Wisdom itself (although the Book of Job is
often classified as Wisdom Literature, it can be treated, for
introductory purposes, as narration). Sometimes it is helpful
to give the general setting, as on the Thirtieth Sunday of Year
B: "The Book of Wisdom was written about a hundred years
before Christ for Jews living in Egypt to call them back to the
basic tenets of their faith." It may be sufficient simply to
indicate the topic, as on the Thirtieth Sunday of Year C:

"Today's first reading teaches us the kind of prayer which pleases God."

D. *Prayer.* For the most part the people are to listen to the readings as being addressed to themselves, but some selections, such as the one for the Sixteenth Sunday of Year A, are addressed to God. It may be helpful to indicate the purpose of the prayer. Often all that is necessary is to give a brief introduction similar to the following: "Today's first reading is unusual in that it is not a teaching which is addressed to us but a prayer which is addressed to God."

When composing an introduction to the readings, do not give a summary or a short homily. Say only what is needed for the people to follow the reading. Do not fall into a pattern of always having introductions for every reading; use introductions only when they are necessary. The introduction may be given by the celebrant, the deacon, or the reader, but it ought to be written out for the sake of clarity and brevity.

Prayer of the Faithful

The Prayer of the Faithful, also known as the General Intercessions, has been restored as an integral part of every Mass. I strongly favor the idea that the homilist should compose the Prayer of the Faithful himself with the help of the parish liturgy committee. Ordinarily this prayer should not be taken from a book of prepared prayers since it should flow from the theme of the day as it is proclaimed in the scriptures and the homily. The controlling theology is that in the Word we hear the good news of God's mercy and love, and through the ministry of our prayer we seek to share God's mercy and love with others.

There are two names for this part of the Mass. "Prayer of the Faithful" reflects the truth that in offering the petitions the people exercise the priesthood of the faithful, which flows from the sacrament of baptism. "General Intercessions," the other name, emphasizes that the prayer is for the benefit of all humanity.

The Presider introduces the prayer. Note that this is not a prayer offered to God but an exhortation directed to the people.

Not correct: "Father, we have seen your compassion in Jesus who fed the five thousand people. We ask you now to show compassion upon those for whom we pray." Correct: "My sisters and my brothers, we pray with confidence to the Father because in his Son, who fed the five thousand people, we see that he is a compassionate God."

The intercessions are led by a deacon or other suitable minister. They may be said or sung, but it should be remembered that the response is not repeated by the people when they are told what it will be, even if it is to be sung. They do not voice the response until the first petition has been offered. As a rule the petitions should include intentions for the needs of the Church, for public authorities and the salvation of the world, for those oppressed by any need, and for the local community. These are not four intentions; rather they indicate the ingredients of this prayer which follows the command of the Holy Spirit as found in the First Letter to Timothy: "I ask that supplications, prayers, and petitions... be offered for everyone, for kings and for all in authority, that we may lead a quiet and tranquil life in all devotion and dignity. This is good and pleasing to God our savior who wills everyone to be saved and to come to the knowledge of the truth" (2:1 ff.).

This prayer of the Mass is to be generous and expansive, rather than self-centered. The intercessions are prayed in union with Jesus who "opened his arms on the cross" to embrace everyone. They express the catholic aspect of Catholic prayer.

Even an intention which is primarily for an individual should not neglect a universal concern. The petition may begin in a particular way, "For the president of our parish council who is to undergo surgery for cancer tomorrow," and then continue in a general vein, "and for all those who are seriously ill, we pray." A good way to prepare the General Intercessions is to read the morning newspaper or to watch the news on television. If anything is calculated to make us aware of human misery and need, it is the communications media. We ought to turn news items into intentions for prayer. It should be remembered that the General Intercessions are indeed prayers of petition, not thanksgiving or anything else. There is a place for every form of prayer during the Mass, but the time of the General Intercessions is reserved for "offering petitions for everyone." Ideally people in their needs, and not causes or projects, are the object of this prayer. These petitions implicitly praise God because they acknowledge his power and his love.

The presider says the concluding prayer, which is not an opportunity for more petitions but an expression of faith and trust. Not correct: "Father, we ask that as Jesus fed the five thousand in the desert so may we find the means to feed the hungry in our country and lead them to join us in our eucharistic banquet." That is a beautiful sentiment but it belongs among the intercessions. Correct: "Father, we have offered our prayers to you because we believe that you never tire of showing your love for us through our Lord Jesus Christ, your Son, who lives and reigns with you forever and ever."

Eucharistic Prayers and Their Prefaces

Consideration of the theme often helps in selecting an appropriate eucharistic prayer with its preface. The First Eucharistic Prayer may be used on any day. The Second is suitable for weekdays; although it has its own preface, it may be used with other prefaces, especially those that summarize the mystery of salvation, such as the Sunday or Weekday prefaces. The Third Prayer may be said with any preface and is particu-

larly suited to Sundays, holy days, and saints' days. The Fourth
Eucharistic Prayer has a fixed preface; no other preface may be
used with it for two reasons: its preface forms an integral whole
with the rest of the prayer after the "Holy, Holy, Holy," and it
is based on the Eastern anaphoras which do not admit of
variable prefaces. The same rule about the preface is to be
followed with the two Eucharistic Prayers for Masses of Reconciliation and the three Eucharistic Prayers for Masses with
Children. As more eucharistic prayers are approved for our
use, they will probably employ fixed prefaces to go with the rest
of the prayer.

The presider may introduce the eucharistic prayer for
the purpose of drawing the people into full, active participation, but always before the preface and never after the "Holy,
Holy, Holy," since the preface is one of the eight elements
which make up a eucharistic prayer. The purpose of the
introduction is not to let the people know which prayer will be
used ("The Second Eucharistic Prayer," or worse still "Please
turn to page 47 in the Missalette for the Second Eucharistic
Prayer"). The purpose is to draw people into full, active
participation through understanding some theme within the
Prayer: ("The Eucharistic Prayer today emphasizes the univer-
sality of God's love" or "Today we praise God for all his
wonderful works in the history of our salvation"). Careful
attention should also be given to selecting one of the four
eucharistic acclamations.

Music

It is not the role of the presider to choose the music but
he should let the musicians know beforehand what the theme
of the day's Mass is and make suggestions for appropriate
selections. Music which is in harmony with the liturgy of the
day leads the people to a devout and deep participation in the
Mass.

Preparing the homily should be the last and most important part of planning. The Sunday homily is the topic of the next chapter.

SUMMARY:

The Sunday homily is the highest from of preaching in the Church. Since it is an integral part of the liturgy, and not an experience in isolation from the rest of the celebration, preparation for it includes planning for the entire Sunday celebration.

EXERCISE:

Following the guidelines in this chapter, write out the elements of preparation for a Sunday Celebration.

CHAPTER XIV

THE SUNDAY HOMILY

"Preaching the gospel is not the subject of a boast; I am under compulsion and have no choice..." (1 Cor 9:16)

Since the restoration of the liturgy mandated by the Second Vatican Council, the term "homily" has been given a technical meaning. Not every sermon which people hear at Mass or during other liturgies is a homily. According to the *Constitution on the Sacred Liturgy* a homily is "a proclamation of God's wonderful works in the history of salvation, the mystery of Christ, which is ever made present and active within us, especially in the celebration of the liturgy" (no. 35). The Constitution goes on to indicate that "by means of the homily the mysteries of faith and the guiding principles of the Christian life are to be expounded from the sacred text during the course of the liturgical year" (no. 52).

The General Instruction of the Roman Missal gives further clarification: "The homily is an integral part of the liturgy... and it is necessary for the nurturing of the Christian life. It should develop some point of the readings or of another text from the Ordinary or from the Proper of the Mass of the day, and take into account the mystery being celebrated and the needs proper to the listeners" (no. 41). Among the forms of preaching, the Sunday homily, which is an integral part of the celebration of the Eucharist, is preeminent (see canon 767 of the Code of Canon Law). This chapter is limited to a consideration of the homily at Sunday Mass.

As with biblical preaching in general (see Chapter XI), the homily is to move from exegesis to hermeneutic, which means that it is to proclaim what God has said in the scriptural message and what he says to us today, or to show what God has done in salvation history and what he is doing now. In the homiletic understanding of the terms, the purpose of exegesis is to make us contemporaneous with God's word; the purpose of hermeneutics is to make God's word contemporaneous with us. Every homily in effect, if not in so many words, proclaims, "Today this scripture is fulfilled in your hearing" (Lk 4:21).

The principles of communication must be followed (see Chapter IV) since "the one who speaks is to deliver God's message" (1 P 2:11). Exegesis unravels the medium so that we may get to God's message. Hermeneutic puts the message into a medium from which the people may shape an appropriate meaning for today.

Homiletic Exegesis

Homiletic preparation begins with the gospel since the liturgy usually intends that the gospel present the theme. Think about the story of the Canaanite woman in Matthew 15:21-28 (Twentieth Sunday of the Year A). It poses something of a challenge to the preacher. A Canaanite woman, not a Jew but a Gentile of an ethnic origin which was particularly abhorrent to the Jewish contemporaries of Matthew, requested Jesus to cure her daughter who was "terribly troubled by a demon." At first Jesus did not respond. When the woman pleaded with him, "Help me, Lord," he responded, in words which are a serious noise factor for us, "It is not right to take the food of sons and daughters and throw it to the dogs." What a shocking thing to say to the poor woman! Some commentators try to overcome the noise factor by observing that the Greek word, "kunarion," means a little dog or a house dog, a pet rather than a mongrel. (Of course it does. One would hardly throw crumbs from the table to an animal which is not a pet in the house.) That approach follows the error of literalism which treats the medium as if it were the message. Unless the audience are those who treat pets as if there were children, they are dismayed to hear Jesus speak to the woman as if she were a dog, little or otherwise.

The Instruction of the Pontifical Biblical Commission of April 21, 1964 gives us the guide which leads us past fundamentalism and literalism to the truth: "The teachings and life of Jesus were not recounted simply for the mere purpose of being kept in remembrance but were 'preached' in such a way as to furnish the Church with the foundation on which to build faith and morals." St. Matthew in this pericope "preached" a truth taught by Jesus in order to build up the morals of the community for which he wrote. That community was still struggling with the problem of the Judaizers, those Christians who maintained that in order to be a disciple of Jesus one had to be or become a Jew and follow the law of Moses. In order to shock his contemporaries into the truth, St. Matthew (as did St. Mark in 7:24 ff.) put on the lips of Jesus a comment which reflected the attitude of some Jewish Christians who looked upon Gentiles as dogs, unfit to partake of the table of the Lord's favor. That attitude Jesus condemned when he said to the woman, "You have great faith! Your wish will come to pass." It was a truth St. Matthew, under the inspiration of the Holy Spirit, wanted his contemporaries to learn.

Homiletic Hermeneutic

The message Jesus taught was that he does not tolerate intolerance, that his disciples must reject no one of good will, and that his Church is to be catholic. St. Matthew put that message into a medium which was well suited to the people for whom he wrote. That message is easy for us to accept if we keep it within the medium of the gospel (I have never met any Canaanites, women or men, but if I ever do I promise to treat them warmly with the love of Christ). But the burden of the preacher is to place that message within a medium which is meaningful for his contemporaries, not St. Matthew's. He is commissioned to expound "the mysteries of faith and the guiding principles of the Christian life from the sacred text." In other words, the homilist must move from exegesis to a homiletic hermeneutic. To do so he needs to know the circumstances of his audience. What are their prejudices? Is a predominantly white congregation hostile to blacks who are moving into the neighborhood? Do blacks in the parish treat all white people as enemies? Is there a conflict concerning Asians or Hispanics? Is there a serious problem because a number of parishioners resent immigrants as "illegal" (as if any child of God could be "illegal"). In the homiletic hermeneutic, the preacher is concerned with what the word of God is saying to us today. It is the most difficult part of composition. A preacher can usually determine a sound exegesis by a study of competent commentaries, but a valid hermeneutic depends on prayer, reflection, and knowledge of people.

First and Second Readings

The first reading (the Old Testament in Ordinary Time) is selected to support the theme of the gospel. On this Sunday (Twentieth Sunday of the Year A) the first reading is from the third part of Isaiah which was proclaimed to the exiles who had returned home from the Babylonian captivity only to find foreigners not of the Jewish religion living there. The reading represents something of a break from the particularism of the past and introduces the idea of universalism: "My house shall be called a house of prayer for all peoples." In composing the homily, the preacher must consider how he will use the first reading to support the message of the gospel.

The second reading in Ordinary Time is continuous and not selective. In the A Cycle the liturgy begins reading from Paul's letter to the Romans on the Ninth Sunday, starting with the third chapter, and continues with selections from that letter through the 24th Sunday, after which it takes up the letter to the Philippians. In other words, the second reading, unlike the first, is not chosen to support or parallel the theme of the gospel. Since it stands on its own, the preacher is not obliged to struggle to make it fit the gospel. He may not even refer to it in his homily, and yet frequently this second reading does conform to the message of the gospel. In the pericope for the Sunday we have been considering, St. Paul warns his Gentile converts against a form of anti-Semitism which is a reverse of the discrimination treated in the gospel. That idea seems to be part of the message of the gospel.

It is not necessary to try to fit the responsorial psalm into the homily, even though at times it may be helpful to the homilist. The psalm is a prayerful response to the first reading and is addressed to God; it is not a proclamation addressed to the people. (That is why ideally it should not be led from the ambo.)

The Message Lives in the Liturgy

Even after establishing a careful exegesis and a sound hermeneutic, the homilist must remember that a homily is part of the liturgy. It partakes of the quality of the liturgy as a reality which is, at one and the same time, past, present, and future. The liturgy celebrates a past event which is made present among us and which contains an orientation to the future. The historical mystery of Christ lives among us in the liturgy and leads us to its fulfillment in his second coming in glory when he will bring the kingdom to fulfillment.

An exquisite example of this understanding of liturgical celebration is found in St. Thomas' *O Sacrum Convivium,* which serves as the antiphon for the *Magnificat* of Second Vespers for the Solemnity of the Body and Blood of the Lord (*Latine dicto, Corpus Christi*). A translation is: "O Sacred Banquet in which Christ is consumed (the sacramental reality), the memory of his passion is recalled (past), the soul is filled with grace (present), and a pledge of future glory is given (future)." A liturgical homily brings the past into the present and directs us to the future. This does not mean that every homily must self-consciously indicate these three temporal aspects of liturgy, nor does it mean that every homily must explicitly refer to the second coming or eternal life or the fulfillment of the kingdom. To do so would be very tiresome. Emphasis should be given to the truth that the message, either of God's words or his actions, becomes a reality in liturgy as the past becomes the present.

As an integral part of liturgy a homily, in the words of the *Constitution on the Liturgy,* is "a proclamation of God's wonderful works in the history of salvation, the mystery of Christ, which is *ever made present and active within us, especially in the celebration of the liturgy.*" Pope Pius XII taught in *Mediator Dei* that "the liturgical year... is not a cold and lifeless representation of the events of the past, or a simple and bare record of a former age. It is rather Christ himself who is ever living in his Church" (no. 165; see also the *Constitution on the Liturgy,* no. 102).

In a homily for the Sunday under consideration, in accord with the liturgical reality, the preacher might remind the congregation that in the Eucharist we celebrate the truth that Jesus opened his arms on the cross to embrace everyone, and that we hear his words, "This is the cup of my blood... It will be shed for you and for all...." The redemptive love of Christ is not limited to a few. Or he might observe that in holy communion Jesus does much more than give the crumbs which fall from the table for which the Canaanite woman pleaded. He offers to all without discrimination the sacred banquet of his body and blood. The point is that what Jesus preached by his words becomes a reality among us through the liturgy. [An example of a complete homily for this Sunday is found in Chapter XVII.]

The gospel for the Thirteenth Sunday of Year B leads readily to a current, liturgical fulfillment of the gospel message. In the story by St. Mark, Jesus was led to the death bed of a girl of twelve. "Taking her hand he said to her, 'Talitha, koum,' which means, 'Little girl, get up.' The girl... stood up and began to walk around." Jesus told his parents, "Give her something to eat." In baptism Jesus has raised us from the death of sin, and he has said to our mother, the Church, "Give them something to eat." The Church responds by nourishing us, her baptized children, with the Body and the Blood of the Lord.

A homilist must be thinking liturgically and realize that his homily is not an essay on the topic or a classroom lecture. It partakes of the beauty and importance of liturgical experience.

Back to Basics

Even after all these considerations, there remains a very important step in homiletic composition. In order to tie all the material together as a unified, coherent, and effective whole the homilist must determine his General End, Statement of Aim, and Central Idea.

After prayer and reflection on the Sunday under consideration, the homilist may conclude that discrimination against an ethnic minority in the parish must be changed by a positive plan of welcome. His formulation becomes something like this: General End, Action. Statement of Aim, "I want my audience to join the parish program of reaching out in welcome to the minorities who are moving into our parish." Central Idea: "Jesus wants us to favor these minorities, as he favored the Canaanite woman." Or the homilist may realize that most of his parishioners must change their outlook on people who are different from themselves. His General End is Persuasion. His Statement of Aim: "I want my audience to agree that discrimination is not acceptable to the Lord." Central Idea: "Jesus refused to discriminate against a woman who was of a race that was hateful to his own people."

The homilist may feel that the General End should be Impression. Statement of Aim: "I want my audience to sense that discrimination is a petty small-mindedness which is unworthy of a disciple of Jesus." Central Idea: "The love of Jesus was big enough to embrace everyone." It may be that the homilist sees in most of his parishioners a naive mentality which fails to recognize discrimination even when they practice it, and so his General End is Clearness. Statement of Aim: "I want my audience to understand that thinking of others as less than ourselves is unacceptable." Central Idea: "Jesus is talking about a form of discrimination which looks upon some people as less than human, as if they were dogs and not children of God."

Doing all the work necessary to arrive at a General End, Statement of Aim, and Central Idea is not a useless exercise. The proper use of these elements shapes the message and puts it into the medium from which the audience can form a meaning which is helpful to them in the Christian life.

Response in Liturgy and Life

When God our Father speaks to us in the liturgy, we should answer him. When we see him act, either directly in the Old Testament or through his Son in the New, we should respond. The answer or the response can be immediately in the liturgy of the day or as we continue in our lives to live as children of God. Sometimes the response is in both liturgy and life, but response does not necessarily mean doing or avoiding something. Response is in accord with the General End of the homily. When the General End is Action, the response is doing or avoiding something and the response will generally be in life, but on the Sunday we have been thinking about it could also be in the liturgy: "We can begin to participate in the program of welcome when in this Mass we are invited to offer a sign of peace to those around us." When the General End is persuasion, the response is for people to change their minds (or at least to be less adamant about their position), and liturgically a preacher may say, "Our petitions in the Prayer of the Faithful today will reflect the kind of attitude Jesus wants to see in us." When the General End is Impression, the response is for people to feel more deeply a truth which they believe. This response could be put on a liturgical level of feelings when the preacher asks, "Can we be petty toward people whom Jesus eagerly welcomes in holy communion?" The response to the General End of Clearness is understanding. The level is that of reason or intellect. Liturgically the preacher might say, "The church becomes really a house of prayer, not just for some, but for all when we are happy that the congregation is made up of diverse groups." Care should be exercised to avoid trite transitions, such as "In a few moments we will all say the 'Our Father' in which we pray in the plural, not in the singular."

Some gospel pericopes offer a model of liturgical response. It may indeed be that the evangelist in these instances, realizing that his gospel would be read aloud in a liturgical assembly, was careful to include in his narrative of what Jesus said and did the reaction of the people as a stimulus to those who were hearing the gospel. When Jesus raised the son of the widow of Nain and gave him back to his mother, St. Luke tells us of the townsfolk that "They began to praise God and to say, 'A great prophet has risen among us. God has visited his people'" (Lk 7:16 ff.). St. Matthew concludes his story of how Jesus forgave the sins of the paralyzed man by indicating the response of the bystanders: "A feeling of awe came over the crowd and they praised God for giving such authority to human beings" (9:8).

Sometimes the model is by an individual, as in the case of the ten lepers who were cured, only one of whom "came back, praising God in a loud voice" (Lk 17:15).

During Ordinary Time the preacher may approach the readings with a feeling of freedom. He is not bound to shape his thinking according to any particular theme. He should allow the scriptures to flow within his mind like a fresh, life-giving stream. Immersed in their vitality he should let them form and shape his thinking. The only consideration he must bring into his reflection is that of "the needs proper to his listeners." During the Liturgical Seasons he must include in his consideration "the mystery being celebrated," as we shall see in the following comments.

Advent-Christmas

Advent has a two-fold character. It looks to the fulfillment of God's plan in the second coming of Christ in glory, and it prepares us to celebrate the birth of the Savior. The four Sundays of Advent in all three cycles follow the same plan. The First Sunday is eschatological. It emphasizes the Second Coming so that we begin the Liturgical Year by celebrating its conclusion. The Second and Third Sundays are devoted to John the Baptist as the herald of the Lord. The Fourth Sunday is Marian in theme and prepares directly for the birth of Christ. Actually only this Fourth Sunday offers much variety in the gospels of the three cycles: the A year is Matthew's version of "how the birth of Jesus Christ came about," the B year is Luke's narrative of the annunciation, and the C year is Luke's story of the visitation. Variety for the first three Sundays of each cycle must be sought pretty much from the readings other than the gospels.

Three Masses are provided for the celebration of Christmas: midnight, dawn, and daytime. It is helpful to note that the readings may be interchanged for pastoral purposes. The gospel for the Mass during the day is the prologue by St. John. I think most people are disappointed to hear this gospel on Christmas day and I find that very few priests are eager to preach on it. A good substitute is the familiar story from Luke which is assigned to the midnight Mass.

Epiphany completes the Christmas season, but Epiphany, which means manifestation, must be understood liturgically to be a threefold feast of manifestation: the first is the revelation to the Magi when Jesus was manifested as the Savior of all people, the second is the baptism in the Jordan when Jesus was manifested as the Father's beloved Son (the original Epiphany feast), and the third is the marriage feast of Cana when Jesus "manifested his glory and his disciples believed in him." The gospel of the marriage feast of Cana appears only in the C cycle after the Feast of the Baptism of the Lord on the Second Sunday of the Year; it is shame that the compilers of the lectionary did not include it in all three cycles within the Christmas season. (See the Liturgy of the Hours for the Solemnity of the Epiphany for a unified presentation of these Epiphany themes, especially in the antiphons for the Benedictus and the Magnificat.)

Lent-Easter

Since the customary forty days of Lent are based on Jesus' retreat in the desert for forty days, the First Sunday of Lent in all three cycles recounts this episode as told in order by Matthew, Mark, and Luke (John omits this event). The Second

Sunday in all three cycles tells the story of the transfiguration, a prefigurement of the glory that will come to Christ through his paschal mystery. On the Third, Fourth, and Fifth Sundays of Lent three specific themes are followed. The A cycle has selected gospels which are related to Christian initiation; when candidates for baptism are present these gospels may also be used for years B and C. The gospels of the B cycle proclaim the paschal mystery. Those of the C cycle are concerned with repentance and renewal. The Old Testament readings are about the history of salvation, traditionally one of the main topics of Lenten instruction. The epistles are selected to harmonize with either the gospel or the Old Testament reading.

Easter is more than a single feast; it is an entire season of fifty days. That is why the Sundays are designated not as Sundays after Easter but as Sundays of Easter. The liturgy during Easter turns from Old Testament selections to the Acts of the Apostles for the first reading. These selections present the life, growth, and witness of the early Church. The second reading in the A cycle is from the First Letter of Peter with its wonderful baptismal themes, in the B cycle it is from the First Letter of John, and in the C cycle it is from the Book of Revelation. As Epiphany completes Christmas, and as confirmation completes baptism, so Pentecost completes the Easter season.

Homilies from the Proper or Ordinary

The usual understanding of a homily these days among most priests is that it is to be based on the scriptures of the day. Although that norm is to be followed on most occasions, the General Instruction of the Roman Missal, in accord with the Instruction, *Inter Oecumenici* of Sept. 26, 1964, clearly indicates that texts from the Ordinary or Proper of the Mass may be a source of the homily. The basic reason for this inclusion is the liturgical maxim, *Lex orandi, lex credendi:* the way in which we pray expresses what we believe. In fact, the deepest expressions of the most vital aspects of our faith are found in the eucharistic prayers (remember that prefaces are part of the eucharistic prayer). It is the duty of preachers to lead people to understand that we have something greater than the catechism or other books for finding the statement and meaning of our faith. That something is the Ordinary and the Proper of the Mass. One great value of preaching from liturgical texts is that people are led to a fuller, more active participation in the liturgy. A second is that they learn their faith more deeply from the indispensable source of the true Christian spirit. [See Chapter XVII for an example of a homily which is derived from liturgical sources other than the scriptures.]

"Taking into account the needs proper to the listeners," as we are told to do in the General Instruction, may lead preachers to conclude that they should preach on liturgical texts. "Taking into account the mystery being celebrated" may also lead preachers to draw from liturgical texts. Two good examples are the Solemnities of the Immaculate Conception and the Assumption, both of which celebrate events which are not found in the scriptures but which are beautifully described in the Prefaces proper to each day, as well as in the other presidential prayers. Some other circumstances suggest a concentration on liturgical texts. An example comes up during the summer months of the B cycle. The gospels for the Sundays in Ordinary Time of Cycle B are taken from St. Mark. His gospel is short, only sixteen chapters, and it is supplemented by the sixth chapter of St. John which is divided over five Sundays, the Seventeenth through Twenty-First Sundays. The theme of this chapter is that we are invited to move from faith in Jesus as Lord to faith in his promise of the holy Eucharist. Careful exegesis can determine a distinct theme from each pericope, but some preachers find it to be stretching matters to preach a different homily for each Sunday from that one chapter, lengthy though it is. One or other of these Sundays seems a suitable time to draw the homily from the Ordinary or Proper of the Mass, without ignoring the gospel. Consider the beautiful content of the Opening Prayer for the Nineteenth Sunday: "Almighty and ever-living God, your Spirit made us your children, confident to call your Father. Increase your Spirit within us and bring us to our promised inheritance." The gospel pericope, John 6:41-51, speaks of the gift of eternal life as the effect of the Eucharist, which is indeed our promised inheritance as God's children. That sounds to me like material from which a true homily is made.

SUMMARY:

The homily is a "proclamation of God's wonderful works in the history of salvation, the mystery of Christ, which is ever made present and active within us, especially in the celebration of the liturgy."

EXERCISE:

Compose a homily for the Sunday which you studied in the previous exercise.

Chapter xv

WEEKDAY HOMILIES

"I am eager to preach the gospel..." (Rm 1:15)

Celebrating a weekday Mass without a homily is like putting a loaf of bread on the table without cutting it for the diners. The General Instruction of the Roman Missal (no. 42) requires that there be a homily on Sundays and holy days of obligation, and recommends that there be a homily on other days, especially on the weekdays of Advent, Lent, and Easter, as well as on other feasts and occasions when people come to church in large numbers. The word "recommends" sounds pretty weak, but one would hope that a priest's eagerness to preach the gospel will move him to give a homily every day. Priests see this hope as reasonable when they come to understand what a daily homily should be.

The first consideration is length. A Sunday homily is to be about seven minutes and should not exceed ten. A weekday homily is to be about two minutes and should not exceed three. An essential step toward brevity is to understand that the weekday homily is not a condensed form of a Sunday homily. The two are different. In the first place, there are only two readings from scripture on weekdays, not three. On the weekdays of Ordinary Time both are continuous selections; no effort has been made to harmonize them. Since they are unrelated to each other, there is no need to cover both readings. Limiting the homily to one is perfectly acceptable. It is usually appropriate to concentrate on the first reading both because it is often less familiar to the people than the gospels and because the gospels usually receive full attention on Sundays, as they should. Actually there are two opportunities to emphasize the gospels even on weekdays since they are repeated every year, but the first reading is on a two year cycle. Sometimes the first reading and the gospel complement each other, but even then the preacher is not obliged to treat them both.

Secondly, there is no necessity for the homilist to include all four elements of a Sunday homily (exegesis, hermeneutic, response in liturgy, response in life). He may be satisfied to give a brief exegesis and say but a few words as a hermeneutic to stimulate the thinking of the people. Or he may judge that an exegesis is not necessary, and so he gives only a hermeneutic. He may relate the message to the liturgy and to life or he may choose to do so only in one instance or possibly in neither, depending on the nature of the readings and the needs of the people.

An Example

On Tuesday of the Twelfth Week in Year II, the first reading is from the Second Book of Kings and tells the story of how Sennacherib intended to conquer Judah. This selection needs some historical background but little else from the homilist who might say something like this:

> Sennacherib, the king of Assyria, had destroyed the northern kingdom of Israel and led the people into slavery. He intended to do fully the same with Judah and so warned Hezekiah, king of Judah. Hezekiah knew that Judah was no match for Assyria. Battling

Assyria would have been like an infant's attempt to ward off the attack of a giant. So Hezekiah did the best of all things. He turned to God in earnest prayer. That night a large portion of the Assyrian army was mysteriously destroyed in its camp. Sennacherib gave up his battle plans and returned to his capital. The Bible does not tell us why so many enemy soldiers suddenly died. Perhaps they were afflicted with some terrible plague. There are two ways of looking at this event. One way is to think that it was just a lucky break for Judah; another is to believe that God intervened to save Judah. The Bible wants to make the point that it was indeed God who acted on behalf of his people. As God's people today we do not live by chance or lucky breaks. We live by the loving providence of our God."

Seasonal Homilies

During the seasons of Advent-Christmas and Lent-Easter, preachers are strongly urged to give a homily each day, more so than on the weekdays of Ordinary Time. The approach to these homilies is basically the same as on ordinary weekdays except that the preacher must "take into account the mystery which is being celebrated" (GIRM, no. 41). A gospel pericope may be used both during Ordinary Time and during one of the two seasons, but with a different emphasis. An example is Matthew 21:28-32 about the two sons who were asked by their father to work in his vineyard. It is read on the Twenty-Sixth Sunday of the Year A, when I find a message with the General End of Clearness on the nature of true obedience, and it is read on Tuesday of the Third Week of Advent, when I am inclined to choose the message that Jesus is the Son who responded in perfect obedience when his Father asked him to come and work in the vineyard of our human world.

For weekdays of Advent and Lent the liturgy does not follow the practice of continuous readings but selects pericopes which are in accord with the themes of the season. The first reading and the gospel are harmonious, at least for the most part, but the preacher should not take this as a sign that seasonal homilies are to be longer than those during Ordinary Time. Seasonal homilies, as on other weekdays, should be simple and brief.

Advent-Christmas

Advent has a two-fold character. From the first Sunday of Advent through December 16th the emphasis is on the second coming of Christ. From December 17th through December 24th the liturgy concentrates on the first coming of Christ and prepares us for the celebration of his birth. This two-fold character is reflected in the two prefaces for Advent. The first is used through December 16th and reminds us that "we watch for the day, hoping that the salvation promised us will be ours when Christ our Lord will come again in his glory." The second begins to be used on December 17th and proclaims that "In his love Christ has filled us with joy as we prepare to celebrate his birth, so that when he comes he may find us watching in prayer, our hearts filled with wonder and praise." These two themes of Advent are not really separable. We should not think that we must preach only on the second coming until December 17th, a practice which would prove to be tedious. It is a matter of emphasis, not exclusivity. The Christmas season extends until the Feast of the Baptism of the Lord which, as I observed in the previous chapter, is part of the Epiphany.

Lent-Easter

The great themes of Lent are presented in no particular order during the weekdays of Lent. They are woven into the fabric of these days which are very important for fostering and nurturing the true Christian spirit. The homilist must keep in mind the three themes of Lent when he is preparing his homilies: the paschal mystery in Christ, the paschal mystery in Christian initiation, and the paschal mystery in repentance and renewal.

The weekdays of Easter highlight readings from the Acts of the Apostles, the gospel of the Church. They present the basic, essential preaching of the Church on the paschal mystery, the death and resurrection of Jesus. They focus on the life of the pristine Church which was empowered by the Holy Spirit, the gift which comes from the death and resurrection of Jesus. The liturgy in this way reflects the Joannine tradition which sees the sending of the Holy Spirit as occurring on the night of the resurrection. Nonetheless, the Easter season does look forward to the Solemnity of Pentecost which concludes and completes the paschal mystery.

Saints' Days

The observance of saints' days admits of different levels of celebration. Solemnities for the universal Church are Mary, Mother of God on January 1, St. Joseph on March 19, the Birth of John the Baptist on June 24, Peter and Paul on June 29, the Assumption on August 15, All Saints on November 1, and the Immaculate Conception on December 8 (the Annunciation on March 25 is a Solemnity of the Lord, not his Mother). These days all have three readings which are proper to the day.

Feasts of saints for the universal Church are the Conversion of St. Paul on January 25, the Chair of Peter on February 22, Mark the Evangelist on April 25, the apostles Philip and James on May 3, the apostle Matthias on May 14, the Visitation on May 31, the apostle Thomas on July 3, the apostle James on July 25, the deacon Lawrence on August 10, the apostle Bartholomew on August 24, the Birth of Mary on September 8, Matthew the Evangelist on September 21, the archangels on September 29, Luke the evangelist on October 18, the apostles

Simon and Jude on October 28, the apostle Andrew on November 30, Stephen on December 26, John the Evangelist on December 27, and the Holy Innocents on December 28. All these days have scriptural readings which are proper to the Feast.

Other saints' days are memorials, either obligatory or optional. Normally they do not have assigned readings but follow those found in the lectionary for the day of the week on which they fall. For some memorials a selected reading is suggested because of some particular relevance to the saint; for example, the gospel from Matthew 18:1-4 which contains Jesus' teaching on becoming a little child is suggested for the memorial of St. Therese of Lisieux on October 1 because she followed the way of spiritual childhood. If a saint's day is raised to a higher level because the saint is the patron of the parish or the diocese, or for some other reason, the readings from the common are to be used (that is the only reason why the lectionary on a saint's day always gives the page number for the common). Otherwise, the selections assigned to the weekday are to be followed since the mind of the liturgy is that the continuous readings of scriptural selections is important for the spiritual nourishment of the people. The liturgy does not want those who celebrate daily Mass to miss out on the scriptures. In fact, when a reading is omitted on a weekday, it may be added to the next day's scripture (see Introduction to the Lectionary, no. VII, 8, d for greater detail on this option).

The homily on memorials which do not have suggested readings presents something of a quandary. Should the homilist forego any comments on the scripture readings and concentrate on the saint, or vice or versa, or should he attempt to harmonize the readings with some aspect of the saint's life? The answer to all possibilities is "yes" — depending on the circumstances. The working principle is that you cannot do everything, especially on a weekday. Often it is surprising how well the readings harmonize with the life of the saint, but it is appropriate to choose either some aspect of the saint's life or to concentrate on one or other of the readings.

The key to preaching on the saints is to remember that the center of all preaching is Jesus Christ because our religion is more than a set of rules or a number of doctrines. Our religion is a person who lives in his disciples. He is the head, and we are the members of his body, the Church. No one person can fully express and live the life of Christ. Saints have done a good job but by necessity they specialize in some aspect of Christ as they allow him to live and act within them. In the zeal of Vincent de Paul, Christ preached to the poor and formed ministers for his Church. In the contemplation of Teresa of Avila, he spent whole nights in prayer to the Father. In the poverty of Francis of Assisi, he had no place even to lay his head. In Peter he was crucified and in Paul he was beheaded. In Maximilian Kolbe, he gave his life that another might live. Christ is not dead; he is alive in the people of his Church. Saints excel in living the life of Christ and it is according to that reality that we celebrate them and preach about them.

It is a burden to preach everyday, but a priest will find that burden light when he incorporates homiletic spirituality into his life and makes the liturgical scriptures the source of his daily meditation. He thereby grows in the indispensable source of the true Christian spirit himself and develops the message which will help his people to do so as well.

SUMMARY:

Even a weekday Mass should be enhanced with a brief homily, especially during Advent and Lent.

EXERCISE:

Compose a homily for a weekday of Ordinary Time, for a weekday of Advent, for a weekday of Lent, and for a saint's day.

CHAPTER XVI

SOLEMNITIES AND FEASTS

"You shall rejoice in your feast..." (Dt 16:14)

Solemnities and Feasts celebrate specific themes which by their nature narrow the interpretation of the liturgical scriptures. A homilist is limited by these themes, but on the other hand when he begins to prepare for these days, he is well on his way in the composition of his homily. There is usually no question of what to preach, only how. These liturgical observances add to the richness of our faith as Catholics, since they are celebrations of "God`s wonderful works in the history of salvation."

The great Solemnities of Christmas and Easter are actually seasons of the year with a preparation, a time of celebration, and a conclusion. Advent prepares for the Incarnation and Birth of Jesus which reaches its climax on Christmas Day and which continues throughout Christmas Time until its conclusion on the Sunday of the Baptism of the Lord. Lent prepares for the celebration of the Paschal Mystery of Christ which reaches its climax in the Paschal Triduum and which continues throughout Easter Time until its conclusion on Pentecost Sunday. These seasons parallel each other in that Christmas celebrates the birth of the Savior and Easter celebrates the birth of the Saved. To put it another way, Christmas celebrates Jesus and Easter celebrates Christ. This is to say that

Christmas focuses on Jesus, the Eternal Son of God, who was conceived by the power of the Holy Spirit and born of the Virgin Mary as our Savior. Easter concentrates on the Son whom God has made both Lord and Christ through his crucifixion and whom he has exalted as Head of the Church (see the preaching in the Acts of Apostles, for example 2:36).

The two central events of Christmas and Easter afford splendid opportunities to form people in the mysteries which constitute the true Christian spirit. Solid preaching at these times can lead people more deeply into the real meaning of our Catholic faith. These opportunities also bring the homilist into contact with a number of people, sometimes a large group, who come to church only on these two days throughout the entire year. A homily which is welcoming and encouraging, and which is well prepared and interesting, contains the grace people need to return to the regular practice of their faith. Although these days are very busy for priests, adequate time must be put aside for proper preparation. As a priest approaches these Solemnities of the Church, working on his homily should be the first thing he does, not the last. Preaching must be given the priority to which the people are entitled and to which a priest is committed by his ordination.

Other Solemnities and Feasts

In the United States and some other countries, the Solemnities of the Epiphany and Corpus Christi have been transferred from weekdays to Sundays (this transfer is allowed only where these days are not holy days of obligation). Outside the favored seasons, Feasts of the Lord replace Sundays. These are the Feast of the Holy Family (Sunday after Christmas), the Baptism of the Lord (Sunday after January 6), the Presentation of the Lord (February 2), the Transfiguration (August 6), and the Triumph of the Cross (September 14). Outside Advent and Christmas Time and Lent and Easter Time, Solemnities of the Saints replace Sundays (a fact which some liturgists judge to be a weakness of the present calendar on the principle that Sundays should always have priority as the Day of the Lord).

Peculiarities of Some Celebrations

Some celebrations are not found explicitly in Scripture. This is not to say that they are not valid; in fact, their presence in the liturgical calendar illustrates the important truth that the Holy Spirit is not limited to the sacred scriptures in the manner in which revelation has been given to the Church. The Spirit continues to work in the Church and especially helps us in our weakness by guiding us to pray as we ought (Romans 8:26). Chief among all forms of prayer in which the Holy Spirit helps us is the Liturgy. For those celebrations which are not explicitly found in the Bible, the liturgy has assigned scriptures which have some appropriateness, but the theme of the celebration is found in the presidential prayers and particularly in the preface of the eucharistic prayer. These celebrations are the Solemnities of the Immaculate Conception (December 8) and the Assumption (August 15) and the Feast of the Birth of Mary (September 8). Of these only the Solemnity of the Assumption replaces a Sunday. These are days when homilies should "develop a text from the Proper of the Mass of the day and take into account the mystery which is being celebrated" (General Instruction of the Roman Missal, no. 41). These days exemplify the important truth which is expressed in Latin as *lex orandi, lex credendi:* the liturgy expresses our faith.

Two Solemnities are unusual in that they propose dogmas rather than celebrate events. These are the Solemnities of the Trinity and Corpus Christi (the Body and Blood of the Lord). In both the Hebrew and the Catholic tradition liturgy celebrates events. This tradition is based on the truth which we proclaim in the Fourth Eucharistic Prayer that all God's actions show his wisdom and love. Liturgy is concerned with the concrete, not the abstract, with salvation history, not theological ideas. (That is why sermons which are merely instructions on some assigned topic are foreign to everything that is going on during Mass.) Some preachers who do not understand the nature of liturgy often say that they are stumped on Trinity Sunday. They protest, "What can you say about the Trinity except that it is a mystery?" Others deem it suitable to give a theological lecture rather than a homily. An approach in accord with liturgical tradition might present the Trinity in a dynamic fashion as God's ceaseless action, an eternal event, of knowing and loving in awesome relationships in which we have been invited to share (and such an approach might lead Catholics away from a spirituality which is almost Unitarian in which many are trapped, which some authors refer to as "Christo-monism"). Another approach could lead people to see more deeply into the Trinitarian truth that all reality flows from the Father, through the Son, in the Holy Spirit, an expression of relationships which shapes the way we pray liturgically.

On the Solemnity of Corpus Christi some preachers content themselves with a dissertation on the complexities of transubstantiation or they proclaim the wonders of the real presence. A liturgical homily on Corpus Christi might present the Eucharist, not as only a static reality, but as the living memorial of the Paschal Mystery, "the sacrament which celebrates the death and resurrection of Christ" (Prayer after Communion for the Seventeenth Sunday of Ordinary Time). Solid sources of doctrine on the dynamic aspect of the Eucharist are the two Prefaces of the Holy Eucharist (Prefaces 47 and 48).

Living the liturgical year with a clear focus on the great Solemnities and Feasts is not only a fulfillment of the truth that we must always and everywhere give thanks and praise to God but it is also employs the proper means for growing in the true Christian spirit. Suitable preaching is a vital part of the Church's mission of "recalling the mysteries of redemption" and of "opening to the faithful the riches of the Lord's powers and mercies so that these are in some way made present at all times, and the faithful are enabled to lay hold of them and become filled with saving grace" (*Constitution on the Liturgy*, no. 102).

SUMMARY:

Some liturgical observances reflect that the Church is not limited to scripture alone, that the liturgy itself is a witness to and a source of truth.

EXERCISE:

Compose a homily for the Solemnity of the Immaculate Conception.

*"God of wisdom and love, source of all good,
send your Spirit to teach us your truth and
guide our actions in your way of peace."*
Prayer from the Tenth Sunday of Ordinary Time

CHAPTER XVII

EXAMPLES OF SERMONS
AND HOMILIES

*"I can speak only what God puts in my
mouth." (Nm 21:3)*

The purpose of this chapter is to present some examples of sermons and homilies which are based on the principles presented in this book. Theory is best understood through observing practice, but these examples are presented with the understanding that the homily is what is preached in the liturgy and not what is printed on a page, and that a homily is directed to a specific audience, as these written examples are not.

1. Doctrinal Homily

The following example is from the Twentieth Sunday of the Year A. The focus is on the gospel which tells the story of the Canaanite woman. The General End is Clearness. The Statement of Aim is: I want the audience to see that rejection of any person is contrary to what it means to be a Catholic. Central Idea: The Church is not an exclusive club.

The Introduction is meant 1) to gain contact with the audience by a Reference to Experience which may be either direct or indirect, 2) to reveal the subject, and 3) to arouse attention.

Little kids often like to form a club with other little kids in the neighborhood. You may have done the same when you were a child. You may even have had a clubhouse of sorts where you held meetings. There really wasn't much of a purpose to the club, but there was one quality which gave it value in your eyes: not everyone could belong. Membership was selective. The fact that other kids were excluded made belonging mean all the more to you. There are people who continue this childish game even after they have grown up. They form clubs with selective membership, with undesirables excluded on the basis of financial status, sex, color, or even religion.

(Transition to exegetical material) Exclusiveness was not unknown in the early Church. The first Christians were Jews. Some of them believed that only Jews could become Christians, while others protested that to become a follower of Christ a non-Jew had to be circumcised and follow the law of Moses. The story in today's gospel was preached in the early Church to correct an attitude of exclusiveness. (Now a reference to the first reading in support of the gospel): This attitude existed despite the clear teaching of our reading from the Old Testament which states that salvation is offered to all who believe in the Lord and keep his commandments. This teaching was fulfilled in people like the Canaanite woman.

This woman was not Jewish. When she asked a favor of Jesus, he insisted that his mission was to the chosen people, the house of Israel. But the woman would not give up. (At this point the preacher must focus the attention of the audience on the gospel without merely repeating the story; an effort must be made to add details and points of interest to the story.) Apparently the woman kept after Jesus. She also attached herself to various disciples who looked deceptively sympathetic for a moment, which prompted them to complain to Jesus, "Get rid of her. She keeps shouting after us."

Jesus resorted to one of his favorite approaches. He told a brief parable which actually reflected the attitude of some of his disciples rather than his own. He said, "It is not right to take the food of sons and daughters and give it to the dogs." There was a sting to these words but they contained a grace for the woman to deepen her faith. With a quick wit, and not a little humility, she responded, "Please, Lord, even the dogs eat the leavings that fall from their masters' tables." Jesus granted her request, and this woman became the fulfillment of the promise from the Book of Isaiah that even foreigners would join themselves to the Lord.

It was a hard lesson for the early Christians to learn, but before long circumstances had become inverted. St. Paul had to write to the non-Jewish Christians at Rome to remind them that they must not boast that they had taken the place of the chosen people of God, that they must not practice their own form of exclusiveness (second reading).

Some people protest that they have a right to form exclusive clubs, but when they want religion to be little more than an exclusive club, we have a situation which is intolerable in the sight of God who does not practice discrimination. The Church of Jesus Christ is open to everyone. It is sad and scandalous when the members of any parish refuse to welcome somebody warmly into their number. They thereby turn aside from the teaching and example of Jesus.

(Fulfillment in today's liturgy:) Jesus invites us to receive him in holy communion. He yearns to unite to himself all who will accept him in faith. How can we refuse to embrace anyone whom Jesus invites to his table? Before receiving the Lord together, we are invited to offer each other a sign of peace. We should offer this sign with sincerity, even if we do not know the person next to us. The sign of peace is a seal and pledge of the unity which is one of the purposes of our receiving the body and the blood of Christ together.

(Conclusion referring back to the Introduction:) It is understandable that children would wish to form an exclusive club, but that is not the kind of Church which Jesus Christ founded and to which we belong. [Adapted from my book, *The Word Made Flesh*.]

2. Homily on the Liturgy

The following is a homily which is drawn from liturgical sources other than the scriptures. The General End is Clearness. The Statement of Aim is: I want the audience to understand that the liturgy teaches us that God is active and present among us according to the manner in which he sent his Son into the world. The Central Idea is: The Liturgy is human and divine like Jesus.

When some people want to find God, they retreat from the ordinary world around them. They try to find peace and quiet in some remote area, far from what they consider to be distractions. Depending on where they live, they may go to the beach or to the desert or some other remote location. No matter where we may live, the liturgy has another idea for us.

The liturgy shows us that God has chosen for the most part to communicate with us through our entering fully into the marvels of his creation, not by retreating from them. God has the power, of course, to act in any way he chooses but he wishes to manifest himself principally through humanity, especially since the incarnation of his divine Son. Jesus is both divine and human; he is God in the flesh, human like us in all things but sin. The liturgy is like Jesus; its divine elements are expressed and communicated through its human aspects.

Think about what happens at Mass. When you look to the altar, you see a man, human like yourself, whom God has called to be his priest. He does not wear secular clothes so that you may see that he fulfills a special ministry: he presides at the Eucharist and he makes our worship possible through a power which can only be understood as divine and which is granted to him in his ordination.

But there is more. Jesus Christ as the worshipper of his Father is present in all the people around you. You must see past their secular dress and their ordinary appearance to believe that Christ is present within them, as he is in you. During the Liturgy of the Word, we could all pick up the Missalette and read it silently on our own, but we should hear Christ speaking to us through those who proclaim the sacred scriptures. Receiving holy communion, God's greatest communication of himself to us through his Son, is never something you do on your own. You could take a host for yourself from the ciborium and pick up the chalice from the altar, but that is not what the liturgy intends. Rather you receive communion, both the Body of the Lord under the appearances of bread and the Blood of the Lord under the appearances of wine, from a fellow human, be that person a bishop, a priest, a deacon, or a special minister.

The liturgy is filled with symbols: the cross, the altar, the ambo, candles, decorations, flowers, and vestments. These and other signs in the liturgy should remind us that God manifests himself through his creation. We must learn to see God's beauty in a sunset, his power in a mighty wind, his loving care in life-giving rain. Above all we must see God in people. God's love is in the embrace of husband and wife, his healing is in those who nurse the sick, his genuineness is in the response of little children, and his joy is in the mutual delight of friends. God's liturgical ways carry over into our other activities. God continues outside of Mass his manner of acting within Mass.

We come to church to find God, and rightly so. But as we are finding God in church during the liturgy, he wishes to raise our minds to a realization that he is present and active all around us. God's will is that always and everywhere our hearts will be lifted to him in praise and thanksgiving for the sharing of his goodness which he is constantly granting to us.

The liturgy teaches us that God is present and active in our world in the manner in which he sent his Son in our world, which is a human, visible, and tangible way. How blessed are the hands which touch him, the eyes which see him, and the ears which hear him. [From my column in the *Los Angeles Tidings* for July 19, 1991.]

3. Doctrinal Allegory

The next homily is from the Seventeenth Sunday of Year A. In the gospel Jesus says that the kingdom of God is like a buried treasure and like a merchant's search for fine pearls (Mt 13:44-46). These analogies are here developed into an extended allegory, presenting the doctrine of fundamental option without using that or other technical expressions. This homily could be called "Prospecting, Christian Style."

Many prospectors came to California during the gold rush of 1849. Any one of them could have related to Jesus' analogy of the treasure in the field. The prospector was a person who had reached an important decision which influenced his whole life. He was willing to risk everything on the possibility of hitting a gold strike which would make him a wealthy man. It

was a decision which required sacrifice and steadfast-
ness.

The first thing this prospector did was to decide
that he was going to base his whole future on the hope
of finding gold in California. He sold his farm in the
Midwest and began the long journey across the Great
Plains, through the tortuous passes of the Rocky Mountains, and over the Sierra Madre range into the Sacra-
mento Valley. It was a difficult journey with risks from
the unpredictable weather and danger from hostile
tribes. Many times the prospector became discouraged and was tempted to turn back, especially as he
came across the bones of those who had succumbed to
the weather or who had died in a gun battle along the
way. But his hope of finding gold moved him to press
on.

When he finally arrived in California, he had to
spend long hours each day mining and panning for
gold. From time to time he grew so tired that he would
go to town and squander his meager earnings on a wild
evening in the local tavern. The next morning, however, his terrible hangover convinced him of his fool-
ishness, and he realized that he had much work to do
before he could really relax. On one occasion he
became so disappointed by continued failure that he
spent several weeks in town doing almost nothing
except drinking and playing poker. All the while he
failed to work his claim. Eventually he remembered his
yearning for gold, and he started all over again. After
more years of many disappointments, he struck a rich
vein. His dream became a reality because he had stuck
to his fundamental decision.

Our lives as Catholics are not unlike that of the
prospector. God has called us to share in the divine life
of his Son (second reading), a calling given us in our
baptism. Our aim is to find the gold of eternal life. At
some point we must make a firm decision that we are

going to work toward the complete fulfillment of
God's invitation so that we may indeed come to enjoy
the treasures of eternal life with him in heaven. That
is what God wants for us.

Our purpose is to achieve something much more
precious and lasting than even the finest gold. We
really have to make up our minds about that. In fact,
the psalm which was our response to the first reading
expressed clearly our purpose: "I have said, O Lord,
that my part is to keep your words. The law of your
mouth is to me more precious than thousands of gold
and silver pieces. For I love your command more than
gold, however fine. For in all your precepts I go
forward; every false way I hate."

It is a long, difficult journey through life, with
many false ways to tempt us, until we reach our goal.
From time to time we will grow tired and discouraged
and squander our spiritual strength on foolish things
- nothing too serious perhaps - small sins of selfishness,
impatience, laziness. Maybe one day we even go so far
as to begin to give up on God. We may be led to such
a state because of the sudden death of a loved one, a
severe financial setback, or perhaps a strong temptation to violate the covenant of marriage or the integrity
of the single state. A serious sin for us is doing what the
prospector did as he failed to work his claim for several
weeks. Deep down, however, the prospector did not
really want to abandon his desire to find gold, as was
shown by the fact that he did start all over again, just as
we, despite serious failures at times, do not really want
to abandon God. After serious sin we have to start all
over again.

Because of our weakness as human beings, some
sins are inevitable. Serious sins should not be part of
our lives because they not only prevent us from going
forward but point us in the wrong direction. Small sins
waste our time and inhibit our progress. Most important of all, we must let nothing, absolutely nothing,

change our purpose in life. King Solomon (first reading) prayed for an understanding heart, for wisdom,
so that he could fulfill his call from God to govern his
people. We are wise people when we know where we
are headed in the journey of life and stick to our
purpose. The journey through life is difficult but we
have the spiritual help of the Body and the Blood of
the Lord in holy communion. Strengthened by this
spiritual food and refreshed by this sacred drink, we
can continue our journey through the deserts and
over the mountains of life. We are prospectors, Christian style. Keeping our faith and hope in eternal life,
more precious than the finest gold, we will find no
sacrifice too great to follow God's will, and one day our
dream will become a reality as we strike the rich vein of
everlasting life. [Adapted from my book, *The Word
Made Flesh*.]

4. Sacramental Homily: Baptism of Infants

The purpose of sacramental homilies is to draw people
into full, conscious, and active participation in the experience.
The sacred scripture for the following homily for the baptism
of several infants is Romans 6:3-11; it is addressed to the
parents, with the others listening and applying the idea to
themselves.

At this moment you parents are making a special
pledge of love for your children. You are concerned
about them as the mysteries and wonders of life are
unfolding before them. Each day, almost each hour,
brings a new experience for them: the sound of voices,
the brilliance of colors, the warmth of soft blankets,
the affection of a caress, the taste of new food. This
moment is another new experience for them, an
experience which will have its effect on them not only
throughout this life which they now enjoy but through-

out the life which lies beyond the grave. This moment is a special pledge of your love and care for your children.

It may sound strange to hear a mention of the grave when life is just beginning, and yet St. Paul writes, "We who are baptized into Christ Jesus are baptized into his death." Through his death on the cross Jesus won the victory over sin. In baptism your little ones will enjoy that victory so that they need not grow up as slaves of sin. As Jesus rose from the dead to a new life in his resurrection, so your children in baptism will be given a new life as children of God.

As you bring your children today to church, to God's home, so throughout their growth you must constantly bring them to God our Father who will now become their Father. In your voices they must hear the word of God as you instruct them and lead to see the brilliance of faith. You must help them to know the person of Jesus Christ, God's Son and their brother, so that they may feel the warmth of his affectionate love. Through you they must be prepared when the time comes to taste a new food, the body and blood of Christ in holy communion.

A big thing happens for your little children today. They receive a whole new life. This day also marks the beginning of your constant, devoted concern for their new life as children of God which they will receive in the sacrament we are now going to celebrate. [From my book, *Living in Christ*.]

5. Sacramental Homily: Marriage

I find it best to direct a wedding homily, or at least most of it, to the bride and groom and allow everyone else to eavesdrop. The gospel for the following homily is John 2:1-11, the story of the marriage feast of Cana, a gospel which couples frequently choose.

Joseph and Mary, a wonderful thing will happen to you in a few moments. You will pledge to each other the great gift of love which God is giving to you. Your presence here in church is a sign that you acknowledge that God is the source of true love.

You are unique among all the millions of couples who have preceded you because you are each the special creation of God, and yet you are like one couple who preceded you. We do not know their names but they are unforgettable because Jesus was at their wedding.

The couple who married at Cana in Galilee many centuries ago were favored to have Jesus as their guest. By his presence in their home Jesus showed his approval of their marriage and he blessed their union. He even followed the custom of giving them a wedding present, a very extraordinary gift, the miracle of changing water into wine so that they and their guests could enjoy the festivities.

But there is no need for you, Joseph and Mary, to be envious of that young couple many years ago at Cana. Jesus, it is true, is not the guest at your wedding; rather, you are his guests. He has invited you here into his home, the church, and he has called you into the most intimate part of his home, close to the altar. He does not merely approve your wedding. He himself will give you a bond of love that will unite you as husband and wife. As you stand hand in hand, his grace will flow from one of you to the other, joining you in a union of loving fidelity.

To show his affection for you, Jesus will give you a wedding present, an extraordinary gift, not indeed water changed into wine, but bread and wine changed into his own Body and Blood to be the strength and joy of your love. He will give this gift to you, not just once only today, but for every time in your lives when you choose to come to the altar together to receive him in holy communion.

This is a day you will never forget. It is a day you can renew with all its fervor and devotion in every Mass you celebrate during your lives together throughout the years. Now, however, do not think of the future. Think only of this blessed moment and of Jesus' concern for you as you are about to give each other his sacrament of marital love. [Adapted from my book, *Living in Christ.*]

6. Sacramental Homily: Anointing of the Sick

The sacrament of Anointing ideally takes place in church within a community celebration for several people. Of course those who need this sacrament frequently are too ill to come to church; in that case every effort should be made to have family and friends present for the anointing since the celebration of this sacrament is part of the liturgy. The gospel for the following homily is Mark 16:15-20.

God our Father is not only the giver of life to us but the source of our well being. Through his Son we see the great concern the Father has for those who are sick. People flocked to Jesus and begged him for a cure for themselves or for a loved one.

We pray to the Father now through his Son because we believe that in the sacrament of Anointing he continues his care and solicitude for those are ill. We have faith in the power and the mercy of God. At this moment you who are ill are very much like the people in the gospels who lived with Jesus and were able to approach him personally. Through this sacrament Jesus spans the centuries and is present to you today.

Part of your faith must be a trust that Jesus knows what is best for you. Perhaps he will choose to remove your illness and make you better. Perhaps he will see fit to strengthen you to bear your sickness patiently in union with his own sufferings on the cross. He may even wish to prepare you now to join him soon in the happiness of heaven. The important truth is that Jesus does not abandon you in sickness or in old age. He is with you in a special way through the sacrament you are about to receive. [Adapted from my book, *Living in Christ.*]

7. Funeral Homilies

The *Constitution on the Sacred Liturgy* (81) states that "the rite for the burial of the dead should evidence more clearly the paschal character of Christian death." Because it is a sharing in the paschal mystery of the death and resurrection of Christ, Christian death is not an end but a beginning. It is through death that we come to the fullness of life. Death is the final physical sharing in the death of Christ which began in baptism and was celebrated in the Eucharist. As Christ was exalted by the Father because of his loving obedience unto death, so we find in our fidelity to Christ the hope of our own resurrection.

Christian death is full of hope, and yet in the celebration of the funeral rite there is a tension between the joy which comes from faith and the sorrow which is the human aspect of a funeral. Death is sad because it means separation, however temporary, and the preacher must respect the feelings of the bereaved. To stand in the pulpit and mouth "alleluias" and expressions of joy and happiness without any sensitivity to the feelings of the people who have lost a loved one can hardly be considered either pastoral or realistic. The preacher must gently lead the people to a firmly founded Christian hope as he follows the transition which is expressed in the Preface for the Dead: "The sadness of death gives way to the bright promise of immortality."

The Church does not wish homilies to be turned into eulogies. At the end of the Mass, family members or friends may express their sentiments and feelings, but the preacher is not to canonize the person who has died. The homily is concerned with the paschal mystery and how that mystery is a reality for the deceased. On the other hand, a homily which is totally devoid of any personal reference to the deceased is cold and distant. Above all, in respect for the feelings of the people, the homily should be brief. The following homily is "general" in that it makes no reference to a specific person who has died. The scriptures are Wisdom 3:1-9 (a text which is frequently used at funerals) and Luke 23:44-49; 24:1-6; a reference is also made at the end of the homily to Psalm 27, the responsorial psalm. The General End is Impression. The Statement of Aim is: I want my audience to realize that for the departed the struggle is over. The Central Idea is: Death is a completion, not an end.

> Today we grieve for our departed friend. We have God's own assurance in his inspired word that the souls of the just are in his hand. God tells us that they are in peace. The struggle is over, suffering has ended, and all yearnings have ceased.
>
> We pray, "May the souls of the faithful departed through the mercy of God rest in peace."
>
> Rest and peace sound very passive to us, like sleep in which there is no activity. But we must not think that in death the joys of life are over. Rather they have just begun. The peace of death is a completion. Its rest is a finish, but death is not an end. We can say that this church in which we have gathered is finished. The building process has been completed. But the church is here. In fact, it was only after the workmen had concluded their construction that the church could serve its purpose as a place of worship. It is in this sense that Christian death brings about a completion, a finish, to earthly existence. With death, and only with death, can the fullness of life begin. It is right that we

give thanks and praise to God in this funeral Mass because for his "faithful people life is changed, not ended," and it is changed for the better.

If we have tears to shed, we should shed them for ourselves who are still on the way to completing life and not for the departed who, like Jesus on the cross, says today, "Father, into your hands I commend my spirit." After Jesus died, the women on Easter morning looked for him among the dead. They looked in the wrong place, since Jesus had risen to new life. We must no longer look for our departed friend on this earth, among those who have yet to reach the state of completion, for now he is gazing upon "the bounty of the Lord in the land of the living." [Adapted from my book, *Living in Christ.*]

8. Easter Homily

The following has been turned into a homily from my column on the liturgy in the *Los Angeles Tidings* for April 20, 1984.

Every person of the Christian faith knows that Easter is a great and joyful celebration. It is also awesome because it is concerned with the ultimate realities of life and death, of faith and hope. In faith we look back upon an event of history, the resurrection of Christ from the dead. In hope we look forward to our own resurrection to the fullness of life. We trust that Christ's resurrection assures our own resurrection, that death will lead to life for us as it did for Christ.

It would seem that if our faith were deep enough and our hope were strong enough we would look forward to death as the gateway to everlasting life, and yet we have an incurable instinct within us whereby we fear death and cling to life.

To have a clearer view of the meaning of death in

the light of Christ's resurrection, think of yourself
before birth in your mother's womb. Let's imagine
that you and your mother can speak with each other
even though you are living within her body. She begins
to tell you about a life awaiting you, a fuller life in the
world outside her body. She explains that you really
ought to look forward to the day of your birth so that
you may begin a more wonderful and complete form
of life. You are not sure of all of this. You say to your
mother, "Wait a minute. It is pretty comfortable where
I am. I am warm and protected, safe and well fed. I
don't know what lies beyond birth and I am not sure I
want it. In fact, I think I will just stay right where I am,
thank you."

Your mother then tries to enrich your outlook by
giving you a motive for hope. She explains, "My little
child, you have an older brother. He lived in my womb
for a time too just as you are doing now. Then he was
born. He has gone before you in birth and, I assure
you, he is doing quite nicely."

Our mother, the Church, through our celebration of Easter speaks to us about our birth into eternal
life. The Church understands that, like birth for an
infant in the womb, death for us in this world is an
unknown. We see what we have here; we are unsure
about what will come after death. God the Father,
through the Church, reveals to us that death leads to
the fullness of life. Death is not the end but the
beginning. That is our faith, and our faith is bolstered
by an image of hope. The truth is that we have an older
brother. He lived for a while within the womb of this
world, but then he died. He has gone before us. His
death was like a birth to new life, a passage to a fuller,
eternal existence. God the Father's plan is for us to
follow him when the time comes for us to leave the
womb of this world.

While we are still in the world, it is vital that we
receive the proper spiritual nourishment. A woman

provides nourishment for the child in her womb. Her doctor warns her: "No cigarettes, no alcohol, no drugs; keep a balanced diet." The nourishment the child receives in the womb is necessary for fostering the health of the child and may even determine whether he will be born alive or dead. While we are in the womb of this earth, our mother, the Church, nourishes us with the Body and the Blood of our brother, Christ. The Eucharist is the spiritual food and drink, richly provided for us in every celebration of the Mass, which helps us grow and develop spiritually and which guarantees a live birth, a birth unto resurrection.

On this Easter day we look back in faith upon the resurrection of Christ, and we can look forward in hope to death as a birth with Christ to the fullness of life. [*L.A. Tidings,* April 20, 1984.]

9. Homily with the General End of Impression

The following homily is for the Twenty-Fourth Sunday of the Year C. The gospel is from the fifteenth chapter of St. Luke's gospel which tells the story of the lost sheep, the lost coin, and the lost son who is usually called the prodigal son. Since the gospel of the "prodigal son" is read in this same year on the Fourth Sunday of Lent, the following homily concentrates on the lost sheep and the lost coin (the short form of the gospel). I have taken the substance of the homily from responses little children gave to questions I asked them during a homily on this gospel (Were you ever lost? What did you do when you were lost? and similar questions), and I have tried to translate their responses into a homily for a general congregation.

When Jesus spoke about a shepherd who had lost a sheep and a woman who had lost a coin, he was not concerned about either sheep or coins. He was concerned about us. He wanted us to realize that we were

that sheep; we were that coin. We were lost in sin and
Jesus came to find us.

My guess is that all of us were lost at one time
when we were little children. It may have been simply
that you were shopping with your mother and you
became separated from her. Since you were young, it
was a frightening experience. Let's imagine that it is
happening to you right now. You are lost in a big store.
You look all around for your mother, but you can find
her nowhere. You ask some people to help you but
either they do not hear you or they are too busy to
bother. Everyone ignores you.

You leave the store and go outside. This is worse
than being in the store because you see many people
walking rapidly along the sidewalk and cars rushing
along the street. No one has time for a little person like
you. Then you look down the block and you see a
church. You think, "The priest will help me." You go up
the steps, raise your hand to door, and pull, but the
door is locked. You go down the steps and across the
street you see a public telephone. Your parents have
made you memorize your home number and luckily
you have some coins in your pocket. You put the coins
in the phone, you dial the number, and its rings - and
it rings, and its rings, and it rings. Nobody answers.
Now you really feel bad. You are desolate. You turn
away from the phone and you realize that all the
people who had been walking up and down the sidewalk are gone. Nobody is in sight. All the cars are gone
too. The street is completely empty except for a newspaper which a breeze is blowing away from you down
the deserted street. You sit down on the bench, you are
feeling hungry, you put your head in your hands, and
you start to cry.

While you are still sobbing and finding it a little
hard to get your breath, you sense that someone is
standing over you. You look up into the eyes of your big
brother. He says, "Mom and Dad sent me to look for

you. Are you lost?" You say, "Oh yes, I am!" He smiles and says to you, "Hold my hand. I will take you home."

We were lost, all of us, because of sin. God our loving Father sent his Son, our brother, to find us and lead us home. That is what it means when we say that Jesus is our Savior. When he takes us by the hand, he leads us to the church which he opens for us. Inside we find people who, Jesus insists, should not ignore each other as did the busy shoppers. They help each other, they pray for each other, they love each other. Through our prayer in church God always answers, unlike the telephone which rang and rang. On the way home to heaven, Jesus does not want us to be hungry; he feeds us with his own Body and Blood. He does not want us to feel lonely or desolate, as if we were no more important than a newspaper being blown down a deserted street.

We are a people who are loved, more loved than was the lost sheep. We are a people who are valuable, more valuable than any lost coin could ever be. We are the people who were lost but who have been found by Jesus our Savior.

EXERCISES:

1. *Doctrinal Homily.* The stated General End of this homily is clearness. What would you have to change and add to make it the General End of Action (see Chapters VIII and XVIII).

2. *Homily on the Liturgy.* Identify the General End, the Statement of Aim, and the Central Idea of this homily.

3. *Doctrinal Allegory.* Identify the General End, the Statement of Aim, and the Central Idea of this homily. Can you arrange the material for a different General End. If so, what needs to be changed or added?

4. *Sacramental Homily:* Baptism of Infants. Using the same

scripture, Romans 6:3-11, compose a homily for the Baptism and Confirmation of adults.

5. *Sacramental Homily: Marriage.* Using 1 Corinthians 13, compose a homily for the sacrament of marriage.

6. *Sacramental Homily: Anointing of the Sick.* Compose a homily for the Anointing of the Sick during Mass at a convalescent hospital.

7. *Funeral Homily.* Using the story of the raising of Lazarus (Jn 11:17-27), or another gospel from the selections for Masses for the Dead, compose a homily for a man who leaves a wife and grown children.

8. *Easter Homily.* Compose a homily to be given during the Easter Vigil.

9. *Homily with the General End of Impression.* Identify within the example given the element of the General End of Impression.

CHAPTER XVIII

THE LITTLE METHOD OF ST. VINCENT DE PAUL

"The revelation of your words sheds light,
giving understanding to the simple."
(Ps 119:130)

A lamentation on the sorry state of preaching is a somewhat constant refrain. Preaching is an extremely difficult art and discontent about its effectiveness has been expressed almost since the day that Jesus said, "Go and make disciples of all the nations... and teach them to observe all that I have commanded you" (Mt 28:1920).

In seventeenth century France St. Vincent de Paul saw a need for a reform in preaching, and his efforts have meaning for preachers today. His development of the Little Method was one means for forming the clergy of his time and was a reaction or antidote to the pulpit abuses which obscured rather than illuminated the word of God. Most of his contemporaries drew their material either from the pagan classics of antiquity or from the rational approach of the scholastics. The use of the classics, often with lengthy quotations in Latin, turned the pulpit into a showplace for erudition rather than enhancing it as the source of edification for virtuous living. Reliance on scholasticism made the sermon, often filled with endless distinctions and definitions, sound more like a dry, classroom lecture than the good news of Christian revelation.

Preachers resorted to histrionics and seemed to ignore the need for propriety in the pulpit. A famous example comes from a seventeenth century preacher known only as "little Father Andrew." On one occasion, he threatened the divine vengeance on women who, as he put it, imitated Mary Magdalen's sinful life but not her penitence. He said, "I see down there a woman very like that sinner. As she is not amending her life, I intend to point her out by throwing my handkerchief at her head." When he pretended to throw his handkerchief, all the women in front of him naturally ducked. He shouted in gleeful self-satisfaction: "Ha, I thought there was only one, and now I see there are more than a hundred."

Some preachers did not hesitate to use the pulpit for their own purposes, while ignoring the word of God. A Milanese priest is reported to have said in his sermon on Easter Sunday in the presence of Cardinal Charles Borromeo, "My brethren, you have a most holy prelate who resembles an Easter egg. He is red, and has been blessed, but it is also true that he is a bit hard."

Vincent's Spirituality

St. Vincent realized that reform of the clergy had to include a reform of their preaching. St. Vincent was a practical man who cherished simplicity and humility. His favorite word for these virtues was "little," and he used it in speaking of the communities he had founded, the Congregation of the Mission and the Daughters of Charity. He referred to both as the "Little Company." And he used the word as the adjective for his method of preaching.

St. Vincent's Little Method reflects his spirituality of simplicity and humility, but it also flows from his practicality. The Little Method is indeed a method. It presents a procedure for developing a sermon, but it also favors a specific content and style of delivery. St. Vincent's practicality was expressed in one of his conferences to his confreres in which we find his exhortation: "Let us love God, my brothers, let us love God, but let it be at the expense of our arms and in the sweat of our brows." He insisted that sentiments of piety are questionable "when they are not translated into the practice of effective love."

In the same conference he said: "Some are content with tender dialogues with God in mental prayer. They even talk about such experiences like angels. But let the question come up of laboring for God, of suffering, of mortifying themselves, of instructing the poor, of going in search of the lost sheep, of loving to be deprived of certain things, of accepting sickness or some disfavor, alas! they are nowhere to be found. Let us not fool ourselves: our whole task consists in translating ideas and resolutions into acts."

St. Vincent's favorite topic was the virtues. He drew his inspiration from prayer, especially as he reflected on the human condition of the Son of God according to the spirituality taught by Cardinal Pierre de Berulle. In other words, he preached the imitation of Christ in accord with one of his mottos, "Quid nunc Christus (what would Christ do now)?" He wrote in a letter to one of his confreres, "Mental prayer is the great book for the preacher."

St. Vincent insisted that simplicity is one of the chief virtues which should be found in a preacher. He advocated simplicity in content, simplicity in language, and simplicity in delivery. He emphasized that the response to a sermon should not be admiration for the preacher but the practice of virtue.

St. Vincent did not, however, disdain emphatic and even dramatic delivery. He was especially adept at mimicry. On a few occasions he felt that he had been carried away and he asked forgiveness of his confreres for overdoing things. He said, "Do not do as I do: crying aloud, clapping my hands and leaning far too much over the pulpit." The great orator, Bishop Bossuet, wrote of Vincent to Pope Clement XI in reference to the Tuesday Conferences for the clergy: "We listened to him with great eagerness, for we felt profoundly that the words of the Apostle were realized in him: 'If anyone speaks, let his words be as the words of God.'"

Vincent urged preachers to imitate Christ in their preaching. He said in a conference: "It was necessary for our Lord first to love those whom he wished to believe in him. No matter what we do, people will never believe us if we do not show love and sympathy toward those whom we wish to persuade."

The Three Ingredients

Persuasion is what St. Vincent made the moving force of his Little Method. He explained the method in a lengthy conference on Friday August 20, 1655 and continued his explanation on Sunday after Vespers. His method consists of three elements: motives, nature, and means (why, what, and how). The motives present the advantages for a proposal, the nature explains the exact meaning of the proposal, and the means indicate how the proposal is to be attained. St. Vincent insisted that it is not necessary to treat these points in order or even to make a clear distinction among them since they are elements or ingredients which make up the sermon.

We do not have records of St. Vincent's sermons at Mass, but we do have written versions of his conferences. In them we find examples of the Little Method. A conference he gave to the Daughters of Charity on June 9, 1658 on one of his favorite topics, confidence in God's providence, provides us with a good model. A few excerpts from this lengthy conference (it comes to sixteen printed pages) illustrate his principles.

Nature: "Sisters, we are dealing here with confidence in the Providence of God. In order for you to understand this, my dear Sisters, you must know that there are two steps, namely, hope and confidence. Hope begets confidence; it is a theological virtue by which we trust that God will give us the graces that are necessary for arriving at eternal life. And this virtue of hope should be enlivened by faith; we should believe without hesitation that God will grant us the grace to reach heaven, provided we make use of the means he bestows on us. Hope then is to trust that God, in his goodness, will fulfill the promises he has made us. To have confidence in Providence means that we should trust that God takes care of those who serve him, as a husband takes care of his wife or a father of his child."

Motives: "The motive which obliges us to trust in God is that we know that he is good, that he loves us most tenderly, that he desires our perfection and salvation, that he takes thought of our souls and our bodies, that he intends to give us all that we need both for the one and the other. — If you abandon yourselves to the guidance of Providence, God will take care of you. He will lead you, as it were, by the hand in the most trying circumstances; if you are ill, he will console you; if you are in prison, he will be by your side to defend you; if you are weak, he will be your strength. And so you have nothing to do but to allow yourselves to be guided by our Lord."

Means: "There are two things you must do: you must persevere in your vocation and you must keep your rules. Providence will preserve you, provided you keep your rules and take care to serve the poor well. For the rest, let yourselves be guided by Providence, even though it may seem to you that everything is about to be lost; you then have all the more reason to trust that our Lord is with you and will make everything turn out for your good. — Say to the Lord, 'I abandon myself wholly to you and cast myself into your arms, as a child into the arms of her father, always to do your holy will.'"

St. Elizabeth Ann Seton, a later disciple of St. Vincent, either by instinct or by design followed the Little Method in speaking to her spiritual daughters. Here is an outline of one of her conferences: "I once read or heard that an interior life means but the continuation of our Savior's life in us.... And what was the first rule of our dear Savior's life? You know it was to do his Father's will. Well, then, the first end I propose in our daily work is to do the will of God (nature); secondly, to do it in the manner he wills (means); and thirdly, to do it because it is his will (motive)."

An Application of the Little Method

We can apply the Little Method to the Fifth Sunday of Ordinary Time, cycle C. The gospel (Lk 5:1-11) is about the great catch of fish. After Peter and his companions had been fishing all night with no success, Jesus told them to put out into deep water and to lower their nets for a catch. Simon protested at first, but then reconsidered and said, "but if *you* say so, I will lower the nets." Following what Jesus told him to do resulted in an amazing catch of fish.

An outline according to the Little Method could be the following: *Nature:* We are called to trust in the word of Jesus. *Motive:* Our faith in who Jesus is as the Lord gives us confidence in him. He can turn bad fishing into good, he can change bread and wine into his body and blood, and he can transform our lives if we trust him. *Means:* even in the worst of situations, when all seems to have failed, we must rely on God.

At times most of the preacher's attention should be given to the motives, at times to the nature but the sermon will not be true to the Little Method and the spirituality of St. Vincent if it is not practical, if it does not set forth the means. St. Vincent insisted, "One should always come down to details. You have seen that. The fruit is there. Descend to particulars, indicate the circumstances, places and times when this or that act... should be performed."

In reading Vincent's conferences one discovers that he could develop the means effectively because he knew what his hearers needed. He understood them and their lives. He was aware of their successes and failures, their joys and sorrows, their hopes and their fears. For a preacher to be successful he must know not only the scriptures but also his people. When he cannot formulate effective motives, the preacher must turn to a deeper study of the scriptures. When he cannot be practical about the means, he must develop a greater attentiveness to people.

The Little Method is not suited to every circumstance or message but, when the sacred text calls for a response in action, Vincent's method is a considerable help in composing and delivering an appropriate homily.

St. Vincent's spirituality shaped the Little Method. A modern preacher can use the Little Method effectively only if he allows that method to shape within him a spirituality of simplicity, humility, and practicality.

SUMMARY:

St. Vincent advocated simplicity and practicality in preaching. He taught that a sermon has three elements: motives, nature, and means. His method is best suited to the General End of Action.

EXERCISE:

Following the Little Method compose a sermon with the General End of Action.

Part III

PREPARATION AND DELIVERY

*"Since I am a poor speaker, how can it be
that Pharaoh will listen to me?"
(Ex 6:30)*

"Speak the speech, I pray you... trippingly on the tongue."

Hamlet, Act III, Scene 2

CHAPTER XIX

THE SPOKEN STYLE

*"I will state directly what is in my mind, my
lips shall utter knowledge sincerely." (Jb 33:3)*

Spoken language, for the sake of the listeners, must be clear and simple. Clarity is necessary because the audience has to hear, understand, and follow what you say as you say it. They cannot go back over your words as one might do while reading a book or magazine. No instant replay is available in a sermon or homily. Simplicity is a quality of good spoken language. It is possible to be more simple in speech than in writing without losing precision or emphasis since the voice supplies subordination, emphasis, and nuances which the written style derives from grammatical construction. Remember that you are not attempting to impress the audience with your linguistic ability or your eloquence. You are trying to present a message in such a way that they can create from it the proper meaning. Here are some practical principles for the spoken style.

1. Avoid long, complex sentences. Use, short simple sentences as much as possible. The following compound, complex sentence is not suited to the spoken style: "Since we are all aware of the old saying that actions speak more loudly than words, it is not surprising that, if a man is supposed to be a good doctor, we are not satisfied merely to hear someone praise his erudition and expertise; rather, on the other hand,

199

we want to see results in a cure." Say simply: "We have an old saying that actions speak louder than words. If a man is supposed to be a good doctor, we are not satisfied to hear someone say how wonderful a doctor he is. We want to see results in a cure."

2. Avoid an inverted order of phrases and the breaking up of direct quotations in telling a story. Not: "I don't know what you are talking about," said the man, scratching his head, "and I feel very confused." Say simply: "The man scratched his head and said, 'I don't know what you are talking about and I am very confused.'"

3. Listen to what you are saying. Preachers are exhorted to mean what they say since they are expected to be sincere. It is equally important that they say what they mean. At the sign of peace a priest said to the congregation, "Now please turn to the person behind you and offer him or her a sign of peace." That direction, of course, does not work. Worse still was the priest who (according to an old clerical joke) on Ash Wednesday announced to the people, "All those from the middle of the church on back will receive ashes in the rear."

4. Make the effort necessary to avoid hackneyed words and expressions; they have been made trite and commonplace by overuse. Some time-honored but much abused expressions are: "tired but happy, too numerous to mention, last but not least, a few well chosen words, time is of the essence, that isn't my bag, let's face it." Often the use of trite expressions is a substitute for thinking so that the expression is not even properly phrased, as in "I could care less." The speaker actually intends to say, "I could not care less." Related to hackneyed expressions are those which convey no significance: a certain baseball announcer often says of a player whom he approves, "I'll tell you one thing, he's some kind of a ball player." Other expressions are redundant, such as "The Lord be with each and every one of you," or "Mass will be at 7:30 P.M. in the evening."

5. Avoid archaic or stilted words and expressions which you may pick up from reading older books, especially those on spiritual subjects, such as: "it behooves us, oftentimes, hence, amongst, thus."

6. Occasionally you may use slang. If you do, make sure that its meaning is clear to the audience, that it is not offensive to them, and that it is suited to the circumstances. It is usually a mistake to try to keep up with current slang, especially that used by youth, since its meaning changes very quickly and because young people do not expect you to use their vocabulary as if you were a teenager.

7. Jargon destroys the beauty and simplicity of language and obscures meaning. In the field of education you find expressions such as: "Learner-centered merged curriculum," and "empirically validated learning package," and the classic "Underachievers and students who have suffered environmental deprivation can be helped by differentiated staffing and elaborated modes of conceptual visualization." Then there is the business man who "introduces innovative techniques" when he is simply trying something new. Some jargon preachers may fall into: "meaningful religious experience, our brokenness, a blessed giftedness, an interpersonal relationship with the Lord." Psychological jargon invaded the language some time ago, and now computer terminology has introduced unhappy expressions. The following is a painful, if ludicrous, example of both: "As we process our fears, we must allow our giftedness to impact our psyche." The damage done by the Persian Gulf was extended even to our use of the English language. The military leaders used what *Time* magazine referred to as "warspeak," an example of which is, "a ballistically induced aperture in the subcutaneous environment," which means "a bullet hole in a human being."

8. Be specific rather than general. Remember the principle of visualization, which was treated in Chapter V, and help people to use their imaginations. General and vague: "I was

sitting at my desk when I heard a horn blow. I looked out my window and saw that a car had stopped outside. Two men got out. One had on a business suit. The other was dressed oddly." The same experience can be reported in words which are specific and visual: "I was sitting at my desk about four o'clock in the afternoon when I heard a car horn blow. I looked out my window and saw that a new, black Dodge had stopped just outside the administration building. Two men got out. One was wearing a blue business suit and a dark tie. The other wore an oversized yellow tee shirt with holes in it and tight fitting white pants, but no shoes."

9. Be concrete rather than abstract, and personal rather than impersonal. Do not talk about mankind or the human race. Talk about people. Do not say, "Man has been raised above the animals through the power of speech"; rather, "We have been raised above all other living creatures on this earth through the power of speech." Not: "A man doesn't have to do big things to be helpful to others"; rather, "We don't have to donate a lot of money or spend a lot of time to be helpful to others." Abstract: "Mortal sin is a grave offense against God; venial sin is less serious." That abstract statement can be made concrete: "Mortal sin tells God that we do not love him at all; venial sin tells God that we do not love as much as we should."

10. Make a deliberate decision about which grammatical person to use in speaking. Often it is appropriate to include yourself by using the first person plural, as in: "St. John in his epistle says that we are all sinners. If we say that we do not have sin, we are lying." It would not be helpful to put that sentence into the second person plural: "You are all sinners, and if you say you are not, then you are lying." Or the other hand, a celibate priest should not speak in the first person plural when referring to matters of which he is not a part; do not say, "When we get up at night to take care of our crying infant, we are reflecting the kind of love God has for all of us." Sometimes the second person plural rather than the first is effective as when

Jesus said, "When you give alms, do not let your left hand know what your right hand is doing" (Mt 6:3). Occasionally you may want to use the second person in order to help visualization: "At two o'clock in the morning you are awakened by the ringing of the telephone next to your bed. You struggle to clear your head as you pick up the phone. You hear an urgent voice say, 'I see smoke coming from one of your windows downstairs.' In an instant you are wide awake and out of your bed."

11. Favor the active voice over the passive. Although the passive voice has its place, the active voice is usually more forceful and direct. To say "We must remember that God loves us" is more effective than "It must be remembered that we are loved by God."

Remember that the spoken style is different from the written style. This principle does not mean that in speaking you need not be precise, correct, and eloquent. It means that proper delivery enhances the composition and that vocal techniques supply for grammatical ones. Correct use of the spoken style means that we "state directly what is in our mind and our lips utter knowledge sincerely."

SUMMARY:

Speaking is different from writing. It is simple, clear, and direct and relies on delivery to serve the purposes of punctuation and other literary devices.

EXERCISE:

Take one of your homilies and read it aloud. Make any changes necessary to turn it into a better example of the spoken style.

Pray, ponder, and produce!

CHAPTER XX

COMPOSING THE TEXT

*"Whoever preaches, let it be with the
words of God." (1 P 4:11)*

Jesus once challenged the people: "If one of you decides
to build a tower, will he not first sit down and calculate the
outlay to see if he has enough money to complete the project?"
He was speaking by analogy about determining the meaning
of discipleship, but his words can make us realize that planning
is needed to construct the tower which is a homily. I confess to
having an inexorable opinion that proper preparation for a
homily is not complete until we can preach without reading
from a manuscript or relying on notes. We need to make up
our minds that preparation is time-consuming but necessary.
Lawrence Olivier said that to be a great actor "one must have
the humility to prepare and the confidence to bring it off."
Something like that applies to preaching.

Reading from a Manuscript

Some preachers carefully type out a manuscript which
with equal care they carry with them into the pulpit. They then
proceed to read the composition to the audience. The effects
of this method are almost always undesirable. Usually there is
little eye contact and rapport with the audience, who for their

part either consciously or unconsciously judge that if the matter is of significance to the preacher, he should not have to read it; it should flow forth from his conviction about the subject and his absorption in it. Others leave behind the manuscript but rely on notes. The effects of this approach are almost the same as those which come from reading a manuscript. When a preacher relies on a manuscript or notes, he has not prepared as fully as he should. Only the most rare occasion justifies reading to people rather than preaching to them, and then the preacher must be careful to compose his homily in a spoken style, rather than a literary one (see Chapter XVIII). I cannot imagine a suitor about to propose marriage, kneeling in the classic posture before his beloved, putting on his glasses, reaching into his pocket for his manuscript or notes, and then reading his deeply felt sentiments to the woman he wants to become his wife.

Robert Frost said that writing free verse in poetry is like playing tennis with the net down. The same analogy applies to reading a homily from a manuscript. It has often been observed in academia that too often education consists in a transfer of material from the notes of the professor to those of the students without passing through the mind of either. Preaching should not be a transfer of truth from the notes of the preacher to the ears of the people without passing through the heart of either. A preacher, filled with love for God and his peoples, must speak from the heart, not from notes.

Memorizing

Some preachers very carefully type out a manuscript which with equal care they commit to memory, word for word. It is very difficult to deliver a memorized homily effectively. The basic problem is that while the preacher is speaking he is remembering, not thinking. Usually memorizing has the same shortcomings as reading from a manuscript. Other problems connected with memorizing are: 1) not having enough time to memorize satisfactorily; 2) being such a slave to the text that forgetting even a word or a phrase stops the homily completely; 3) coming across as stilted because the homily "sounds" memorized; 4) being so glued to the text that adaptations are impossible while speaking; 5) remaining distant from the audience. Actors must rely on memory but preachers should rely on conviction.

Suggested Method

Each preacher eventually develops his own method of preparation. I suggest here a method which you may find helpful as a total approach or which you may use as a starting point for your own. I review the liturgy of the day in a prayerful spirit, and I consult appropriate commentaries and other sources. After I have derived a message from the liturgy, I am careful not to try to put something in writing too soon. I like to brood over the message in relationship to the people to whom I am going to preach. I dismiss no ideas at first; I simply allow all the thoughts which are in my mind either from recent research or habitual knowledge to play upon one another (I like to go for a walk at this time). Gradually I begin to develop something specific. I come to a point when I can decide upon a General End and I can formulate a Statement of Aim and a Central Idea.

Next I jot down an outline in a very informal way. I simply put down on paper anything which helps me to see the sequence of ideas — it may be a series of words or phrases mixed with a few sentences. I call this the compositional outline. Now I am ready to compose a manuscript. Writing a manuscript helps me to clarify my thinking and forces me to find appropriate words for what I want to say. Sometimes I omit this step, especially when the development of the homily is very clear in my mind. In fact, I must admit that after years of preaching I rarely type out a complete manuscript, and yet there are times, especially when my thinking is vague on a subject, when I find it very helpful to go back to composing a complete manuscript.

After I have composed the manuscript, or thought through the homily, I make a second outline which I call the speech outline. Again it is informal — it is anything which helps me to see the sequence of thoughts. I formulate an introduction and conclusion around the outline and I fix all that in my mind. I am now ready for more brooding. Only infrequently do I now practice a homily aloud, but younger preachers probably should do so, especially with a recorder. Practicing a homily aloud too many times can deaden the delivery since the homily may lose its freshness. On the other hand, I have found that I can go over the homily many times in my mind without losing that sense of freshness.

A Visual Approach

Of course a preacher who is urged not to read from a manuscript or to rely on notes is afraid that he is going to forget what he wants to say. My colleague in homiletics at St. John's Seminary, Father Michael Roebert, has developed a method to allay such fears. He here explains that method:

"In effective preaching, communication occurs when there are no notes or manuscript at hand to come between the preacher and the listeners who are also viewers. To maintain constant eye contact and direct rapport means that the preacher must be able to scan his 'brain screen' to recall what is to be said. What is desired is not memorization of the exact text but rather the picturing of the bare bones of the outline of main thoughts which the preacher will flesh out in an extemporaneous manner. This gives the quality of conversation with the audience, rather than 'preaching at' the listeners.

"If the brain is forced to recall many specific details and

single thoughts, the brain generally becomes nervous and cannot handle this pressure. With the least distraction, the brain decides to close down, to go south for the winter, and stops the motor. The speaker goes blank. For most ordinary mortals there needs to be a method of recall which does not overload the system, a method of withdrawal which does not break the bank. Consider the following. Most of us have little difficulty recalling a picture. The brain loves pictures.

"Here is a way to create a picture of a homily. Visualize a window frame divided into four sections. Divide the talk into four parts such as 1) introduction, 2) common experience or connection with central idea, 3) scriptural or topical application to central idea, 4) application and conclusion. This fourfold breakdown might simply be introduction, central idea, application, and conclusion. Now think of four tangible objects or key words which can trigger the thoughts in each section. For example, a brief weekday homily on the Exaltation of the Holy Cross might develop something like this: Introduction: trees give shade, help protect the soil and environment, produce and purify the air and protect the ozone; Common Experience: Even with all the modern materials for construction, carpenters state that wood is still the best, flexible material to work with for lasting results; Scripture or Topic central idea: We honor the tree of the cross as the source of our strength and assurance of victory. God gives us the cross of our lives as material to work with in building our lives. Conclusion: Allow the Risen Lord Jesus working through the cross to give us the pure air and cool shade of his Spirit in this eucharistic celebration.

"For this homily on the Exaltation of the Cross, recall four images: in the first box picture a tree, in the second box a hammer, in the third a cross, and in the fourth Jesus, ourselves, and a cross. Or simply picture one word in each box: tree, carpenter, exalt, spirit. Or even more simply picture three letters: T, C, E, S.

"The usefulness of this method or something similar is that it lets the brain relax by needing to recall only single pictures, words, or even letters. In this fashion when the speaker hits the agony of going blank, he can move on to the next picture. Often such ease in moving on allows the brain to pick up the missing ideas and thread them back into the homily. This peace of mind allows the Spirit to work more effectively and creatively."

I thank my colleague, Father Michael Roebert, for presenting his method of retention, which has proven helpful and calming for many of our students.

A perceptive woman once told me that she finds that there are two kinds of preachers, those who speak from the head and those who speak from the heart. Reading from a manuscript or relying on notes seems to be speaking from the head. Preaching a homily should be a matter of speaking from the heart. We need to know what we want to preach by heart, not in the sense that we have memorized it, but in the sense that we have made it part of our deep convictions.

SUMMARY:

The message is to be considered in relationship to the audience, the occasion, and the time limit. Begin with an outline, do a manuscript, end with an outline which includes a complete introduction and conclusion. Memorize the introduction and conclusion and the outline. Use language which is simple, direct, clear, and concrete. Practice aloud and silently. Do not read from the manuscript. Do not use notes.

EXERCISE:

Try practicing the method of retention which is presented by Father Michael Roebert in this chapter.

CHAPTER XXI

ORAL INTERPRETATION AND DELIVERY

"Ah, Lord God... I know not how to speak."
(Jr 1:6)

The Bishops' Committee on the Liturgy has insisted that "All scripture readings are to be proclamations, not mere recitations" ("On Praying and Reading in the Vernacular," 1969). The proclamation of the scriptures during the celebration of the liturgy should follow the principles for oral interpretation.

Nature of Oral Interpretation

Oral interpretation is the art which communicates the meaning of the printed page by means of reading aloud. As its name indicates, it includes two aspects: interpretation and oral communication. The black marks on a page which we call words are symbols. They stand for the ideas and feelings of the author as he wishes to communicate them to others. It is for the oral readers to determine the meaning of these symbols in their full sense. They must consider both the denotation and the connotation of the words. They must understand their intellectual meaning and their emotional values. They must try to determine not only why the author has written what he

211

has written, but they must also investigate why he has chosen to omit what he has omitted.

Interpretation of the scriptures should follow all the canons of scriptural criticism. Put as simply as possible, interpreters must consider the literary form of the scriptural pericope, the historical setting, the intention and style of the author, and the understanding of the Church. Fortunately we are blessed with excellent scriptural commentaries; a good place to start is with one of two works I have already mentioned, *The Collegeville Bible Commentary* or, for a more extended treatment, *The New Jerome Biblical Commentary*.

Unlike literary critics, oral interpreters do not express their understanding by writing or lecturing about the selection. They communicate their interpretation by reading the text aloud. But they are not actors. In acting the performer becomes the character. A Shakespearean actor says in effect, "Look at me. I am Hamlet." On the stage the actors transform themselves through costumes and makeup. They want the audience to think only of the character and to forget their true identity. They ask of the audience the kind of poetic faith of which Coleridge wrote, a willing suspension of disbelief. They want the audience to accept that what they are witnessing is reality taking place before their eyes. Since the play is presented, not to the audience, but before the audience, actors are usually directed to disregard them.

In contrast to the approach followed by actors, oral interpreters retain their own personality. They become a medium, a mediator for the author. They do not impersonate, but only reflect characters; they do not act, but only suggest emotions. They are acutely aware of their audience and read directly to them. Oral interpretation has its own place as an art form but it has a special role in the sacred liturgy. Readers during the liturgy, including the ordained ministers who proclaim the gospel, stand at the ambo to present an oral interpretation of the scriptures.

Most bishops, priests, and deacons do not want to come across as "hams." As a consequence, many tend to read with but little feeling. We must become convinced that oral interpretation is the happy middle ground between acting and reciting. Think of the story of Bartimaeus, the blind beggar (Thirtieth Sunday of the Year B). Few emotions in the gospel are more poignant or more urgently expressed than the cry of this blind man who pleads with Jesus to let him see. An actor, his eyes filled with tears and his voice shaking with uncontrollable desire, would shout in loud desperation, "JESUS, SON OF DAVID, HAVE PITY ON ME!" An uninvolved reader, with no more emotion than a napping kitten, would recite the words flatly, "Jesus, master, have pity on me." An oral interpreter is somewhere between these two extremes: he suggests the emotional plea without impersonating the blind man. Oral interpretation does justice to the composition.

Let it be clear, then, that oral interpreters at the liturgy are not actors; they are ministers. They do not wear costumes; they are clothed (I hope) in the white garment of baptism, the alb, which is a sign of ministry (see no. 298 in the *General Instruction of the Roman Missal*). They are a mediator for the author of sacred scripture, the Holy Spirit.

Analysis of A Gospel

A simple step by step process helps the ordained minister to prepare for an oral interpretation of a gospel pericope. This method will aid also in preparing the homily. I suggest seven steps in the analysis of a gospel pericope: 1) What is the *Message?* Express it to yourself in a sentence. 2) What are the *Techniques* or devices which the author uses to communicate his message? 3) What are the *Transitions*, the changes in pace, moods, scenes, or persons? 4) What are the *Emotions* or feelings of the principal characters of the action? 5) What is the *Mood* or spirit of the whole pericope? 6) What is the *Climax* or high point of the presentation? 7) What is your own *Reaction* to the pericope?

Example from the Tenth Sunday of the Year, C

The straightforward gospel for the Thirtieth Sunday of the Year in the C cycle, the parable of the two men who went up to the temple to pray, serves as a good subject of analysis. 1. The *Message* is that God is pleased with honest, humble prayer. 2. The *Techniques* are these: there is a contrast between the Pharisee and the tax collector; the Pharisee betrays his pride by his own words; the tax collector manifests his humility. The Pharisee speaks in a loud voice to make sure that God hears him and he probably hopes that others in the temple will hear him too; the tax collector is soft spoken, and this suggests his humility. 3. The *Transitions* are: a change from Jesus the narrator to the persons of the Pharisee and the tax collector and back to Jesus who applies the message. 4. The *Emotions* are: Jesus is calm as the teacher, the Pharisee is haughty, and the tax collector is modest. 5. The *Mood* is quietly didactic. 6. The *Climax* comes in the application by Jesus, "Believe me, this man went home from the temple justified but the other did not." 7. My *Reaction* is that I am moved to examine my own attitudes toward others and how these attitudes are reflected in my prayer.

Other Examples

On the Twenty-Fourth Sunday of the Year in Cycle A we hear a parable which is expert in its use of *Techniques*. The parable answers Peter's question about forgiveness. One official owed a huge amount, the other owed only a mere fraction of that debt. When the first official asked the king to be patient with him, the king granted more than he asked and wrote off the debt. This official then went out and acted in a contrary fashion. When a man who owed him a very small amount asked him to be patient, he would hear none of it. Oral reading should stress these techniques. *Emotions* also play a significant part in the parable as the king is compassionate and understanding and then angry. The change in emotions is also a good example of *Transitions*. The *Climax* is the demand of the king, "Should you not have dealt mercifully with your fellow servant, as I dealt with you?"

Most pericopes admit of multiple interpretations, or at least varied points of emphasis, but any interpretation must be based on sound exegesis. Determining the message affects all the other points of interpretation. On the Fourth Sunday of Easter in the B cycle Jesus proclaims that he is the Good Shepherd. One *Message* is that Jesus loves us so much that as our Shepherd he lays down his life for us. In accord with this message the *Climax* is the words of Jesus, "For these sheep I lay down my life." *Techniques* are the contrast between the shepherd who lays down his life for his sheep and the hired hand who runs away at the sight of danger. On the other hand, another *Message* is that Jesus wants to bring about the unity of his followers. In this case the *Climax* is "There shall be one flock then, one shepherd." One *Technique* in this interpretation is that when the hired hand runs away, the wolf comes and snatches and scatters the sheep. That is why a good shepherd is needed to defend against forces intent on scattering the sheep in order to devour them.

This process of analysis can be used for narrative pericopes from the Old Testament. It can also be used with slight changes for other types of pericopes which are read during the liturgy.

Analysis guides the reader to identify the techniques so that he may emphasize them — if everything is emphasized, then nothing is emphasized. It helps him to know which emotions to suggest, which mood to sustain, and which transitions to mark — if everything sounds the same, then justice is not done to the artistry of the pericope. It leads him to the climax — if there is no stress upon the high point of the narrative, then it seems no more important than anything else in the reading. Analysis helps the reader to have a personal appreciation of the pericope by asking him to express his reaction to the gospel reading. An analysis is of value to the degree that it influences the reading aloud of the pericope. Oral interpretation occurs when analysis and proclamation meet.

The Vocal Factors

The oral interpreter has an instrument, the human vocal mechanism, to express his interpretation. This wonderful mechanism is controlled by what are called the vocal factors. Every oral interpreter must take these factors into account and use them in the proper fashion. The same factors, it may be added, make up the delivery of the homilist. There are seven of them.

1. *Volume* or force. This means simply loudness. The first question is, "Can I be heard?" but there are other considerations. Good volume helps articulation and enunciation. When you sense that your delivery is lifeless, very often increasing the volume will bring about a more energetic presentation. Changing the volume can communicate meaning, especially the relative importance of ideas. Increased volume is often an effective emphasis for a climactic idea but it should be remembered that the other vocal factors may at times be a more appropriate means for gaining emphasis.

2. *Rate* refers to the amount of time it takes you to say a given number of words. The rate must be slow enough to allow the audience to hear distinctly every word and syllable that comes from your mouth. Never make the audience guess at

what a word is or force them to get it from the context. Variations in rate may be used to express meaning, to achieve emphasis, or to gain variety.

3. *Pause* is the lack of sound between words, phrases, or sentences. It is used to gain emphasis or to mark transitions. It is also a vocal form of punctuation, but regardless of the punctuation in a scriptural pericope or other text, you should pause when it helps to convey the right meaning or to give the proper emphasis. Pausing briefly at the right moments also gives the audience an opportunity to reflect on what they are hearing.

4. *Quantity* means the duration of sound in the utterance of vowels, syllables, and words. Some words have long quantity by nature; e.g., pool, dale, reel. Some words have short quantity by nature; e.g., bit, kid, pup. You should ordinarily follow the natural quantity, but sometimes you may increase or decrease the natural quantity to achieve a particular effect. A common fault to be avoided is the unnatural quantifying of syllables which results in an affected, and somewhat pompous form of delivery. Some readers seem to think that quantifying lends dignity to a scriptural reading, but they are mistaken.

5. *Pitch* refers to the musical note you hit when you utter a sound. The normal speech range is about five notes, but many do not use even this five note span. Most speakers and readers need more range in their pitch span. You should, however, speak for the most part in the middle of your range in a natural, unforced manner.

6. *Melody* in speaking or reading aloud means the movement of the voice up and down the scale in different inflections in order to express various meanings and feelings. Melody comes about through the relationship of notes to one another. Proper melody is necessary for communication, for avoiding monotony, and for holding attention. It is easier to

say what to avoid regarding melody than to indicate which melody you should create: A) Song notes. When you unduly quantify a syllable, you create a song note. A series of song notes results in what many people call "a sing-song" delivery. B) Melody pattern. This means the arbitrary pattern of recurring pitches used by some preachers and political orators, and usually includes song notes. The result is monotony and boredom. C) Insufficient melody. Sometimes people say a person speaks in a monotone. This means that the speaker employs insufficient melody.

7. *Projection.* This means, as many speech teachers say, "throwing the voice." Although it is not the same as volume, it usually includes an increase in volume and a slight elevation of pitch. Projection is necessary when you are speaking or reading to a large audience.

All of the vocal factors come into play when you utter even a simple sentence. One factor cannot be isolated from the another, except in the case of practice, and all of them must be used together for effective speaking and reading. One of the best helps to a proper use of the vocal factors is to listen to yourself on either an audio or video tape recording.

The vocal factors are driven by the vocal mechanics which include proper breathing, phonation (production of sound), resonance, articulation, enunciation, and pronunciation. It is very difficult to learn the correct use of mechanics from a book; if you have a problem in any of these mechanics, do not hesitate to consult an expert.

Conversational Style

Good preaching and reading aloud employ a conversational style. This does not mean that you preach or read in exactly the same way in which you carry on a conversation. It means that you use the best qualities of good conversation and you avoid the faults which are common in conversation. Some good qualities of conversation to be preserved are: spontaneity, simplicity, sincerity, ease, intimacy, eagerness, natural language, expressive melody, flowing speech, and personal warmth. Some bad qualities to be avoided are: insufficient volume, too rapid and uniform rate, too few pauses, insufficient melody, poor articulation, very informal language, low energy, and vocalized pauses.

Opposed to conversational style are the oratorical style and the ministerial style. Oratorical style tends to be pompous with soaring melody and extremes in volume. It usually calls attention to itself rather than to what is read or said. Ministerial style employs melody patterns without any particular relationship to content. It usually fails to communicate effectively.

What is most appropriate for a priest and or other minister is to be your true self. There should not be a pulpit personality distinct from that person who speaks openly and lovingly to people who are closest to you. Conversational style, correctly understood and properly employed, presents your true self at your best.

SUMMARY:

Oral interpretation is not acting. It consists in suggesting characters and their emotions rather than impersonating them. Delivery is integral to preaching since a homily is not words on a page; a homily is the spoken word.

EXERCISE:

Do an analysis of any Sunday gospel and record your oral presentation of it. Listen to your recording to judge whether your presentation expresses your analysis.

APPENDIX

*"Be not the first by whom the new is tried,
Nor yet the last to lay the old aside."*

Alexander Pope

SUGGESTIONS FOR A CURRICULUM IN HOMILETICS

"By means of many parables he taught them
the message in a way they could understand."
(Mk 4:22)

Teaching homiletics can be rewarding simply because of the importance of preaching in the Church. It can also be frustrating because so many aspects of preaching are beyond teaching. Theology and method can be taught, but a preacher needs native talent and ability. There is some truth in saying that a preacher is born, not made, but there is consolation in knowing that any degree of talent can be refined and any amount of ability can be enhanced.

A significant aspect of teaching homiletics is that preachers come to a class already formed, for good or for ill. It is not the person of mature years alone who preaches. The infant preaches, the child preaches, and the adolescent preaches. We begin to be formed as preachers from the time we were conceived when our talents were contained in the genes we inherited, and the womb became the first environment of many which would help to shape our personality and our abilities. I wish I could return every student to childhood and tell him, "Read, study, reflect. Neglect nothing. Everything you learn you will use somehow in preaching. Love language.

Develop vocabulary. Use your imagination. Accept love and affection from God and his people, and return love and affection gratefully. Be a 'people person.' Live with God in his world."

Remedial work is very difficult. It is almost impossible to make up for what was lacking to a person while he was growing up but we must try. Students must be encouraged to read widely, to reflect deeply, to listen attentively, and to practice their writing and speaking skills. They are to be helped to see how every class they take in the seminary can be related to homiletics, whether the professor makes the effort to do so or not. They are to be urged to develop homiletic spirituality and to pray in an apostolic spirit (see Chapters II and III). Aristotle in his *Rhetoric* emphasized that the character (ethos) of the speaker is the most potent means of persuasion. In a preacher *ethos* is properly translated as holiness, and the preacher who does not live in union with Christ and who does not love his people will never be the instrument of God's communication for which he was ordained.

A Progressive Approach

Homiletics is concerned with developing sound habits. By their nature, habits are formed by the regular and uninterrupted repetition of acts. For this reason I advocate the principle of gradualism in the arrangement of courses. An intense program, say of six units over two semesters, cannot be as effective as six units over six semesters. It is much better, in other words, to have six one unit courses than two courses of three units each. Deans may not like the inconvenience of scheduling one unit courses, and some representatives of accrediting associations object to one unit courses because of their lack of expertise in matters homiletic, but I can attest that experience has taught me that gradualism is more effective than intensity. It not only develops habits of delivery but also

habits of thinking homiletically. It also assists in applying
theological and scriptural courses to homiletics while they are
being taken.

In the ideal a student who is beginning homiletic studies
has already had courses in oral interpretation, delivery, and
speech composition. If he has not, some make-up work is
necessary. This is not to say that homiletics rests secure when
students have had previous training. Because good habits are
formed slowly and must constantly be refined, the homiletics
professor will discover, as does even a coach of professional
football players, that he must have recourse to fundamentals
over and over.

Class Activities

The goal of any homiletics course is not to have the
student give as many sermons or homilies as possible. As my
brother, Father Oscar Miller likes to say, practice does not
make perfect; practice only makes permanent. Every course
should be a wedding of theory and practice. The instructor
must give constant guidance and direction. Comments on
presentations should be both positive and negative because it
is just as important for a student to know what he is doing right
and why, as it is for him to know what he is doing wrong and
why, both in content and delivery. In other words, a student
should know both his strengths and his areas for growth.

Some object that students should never give practice
sermons to imaginary audiences, that they should preach
"real" sermons to their own classmates. This proposal is based
on false premises. The first is to think that it is impossible to
talk to an unseen audience, but everyone knows that radio and
television personalities do so all the time. A second false
premise is to assume that seminarians will easily make the
necessary transition in style and content when the time comes
to preach to lay congregations. The fact is that one of the

greatest needs in preaching today is for priests to present the gospel within the context of people's lives in simple, concrete language, to address everyday problems, and to use practical, current examples and illustrations as Jesus did. Seminarians must be lifted beyond the theological language which they hear and speak in classes, which may be acceptable in sermons and homilies which are preached to the seminary community, but which are quite inappropriate in those which are meant for lay congregations. Field education is of great assistance to homiletics in this regard.

All this is not to imply that seminarians do not make good critics for each other. In fact, often seminarians are better critics than non-seminarians because they know what a fellow seminarian should be doing. It is important, especially during internship, that seminarians receive criticism from a lay group, but this group needs instruction about the nature and purpose of homilies, otherwise preachers may receive inappropriate suggestions, such as "It would be nice on the Sundays of October for you to preach a series on the Blessed Mother," or "Abortion is such an evil that you should preach about it every Sunday."

Curriculum

"Among the forms of preaching, the homily is preeminent; it is part of the liturgy itself." So states Canon 767. The homiletic curriculum should not begin with liturgical homilies but lead up to them as the summit of preaching through the practice of other forms of sermons. Of vital importance is the integration of theology courses with homiletics. We should urge professors to relate their subjects to homiletics in the spirit of homiletic spirituality, but whether they do or not, the professor of homiletics should insist that seminarians draw their material from their theological courses and "translate" that material into homiletic language. It is surprising how many seminarians, and even priests, tend to depend on what they learned in catechism as children and to approach scripture as literalists. Theological and scriptural studies seem to be relegated to some hidden crevice of their minds. Preachers must be schooled to draw from deeper sources.

Over the years I have tried many approaches to homiletics, always searching for the perfect curriculum and treatment. Each professor will find from experience the most efficient program in particular circumstances, and no one approach should be imposed on everyone, but I propose here a general plan which can be modified or amplified, taking into account the constraints of a crowded curriculum. I hope that as a minimum we can have six, one unit courses.

First Course

This course covers principles of delivery and oral interpretation (see Chapter XXI). There should also be opportunities for extemporaneous speaking. The goal should be that the students proclaim scriptural pericopes well and speak in a natural, but purified, style. Learning to tell stories is an important part of this course.

Second Course

After the course on delivery and oral interpretation, the students are ready for homiletic theory. This course covers the material in the first nine chapters of this book. Although there should be some opportunity for the students to give sermons in class, the concentration should be on fundamental theory which should guide all subsequent classes. This is the most important course in homiletics.

Third Course

I suggest concentration first on sermons with the General End of Action (since that is usually the easiest General End to handle), then on sermons on modern problems (e.g. social justice, war and peace, abortion, violence, and drugs) since these issues must be addressed both within homilies and during other opportunities, and lastly presentations to ecumenical groups for the sake of developing awareness of the audience. These types are valid in themselves and also reflect aspects of liturgical homilies. If the number of units allowed for homiletics must be reduced, this course could be an elective.

Fourth Course

The fourth course builds toward an experience with a liturgical homily in the strict sense. It begins with sermons on doctrinal subjects (see Chapter X), moves to biblical preaching (chapter XI), and concludes with Sunday homilies (Chapter XIV).

Fifth Course

This course should precede internship and prepare for it. In class students should give witness talks and instructions in accord with the law for lay preaching (canon 766) since preaching should be an important part of their experience as interns. They should also learn the principles of preparation for liturgy (see Chapter XIII) and practice daily homilies (see Chapter XV).

Sixth Course

This course should follow internship. It should allow opportunities for the seminarians to reflect on their experience of preaching during the internship in order to determine what they need to work on, but it should also progress through new homiletic practice, especially for Solemnities (see Chapter XVI) and for sacramental celebrations (see Chapter XII).

Whenever decisions are being made about courses in homiletics, those responsible should keep in mind this principle from the Code of Canon Law: "Since the people of God are first brought together by the word of the living God, which it is altogether proper to require from the mouth of priests, sacred ministers are to value greatly the task of preaching since among their principal duties is the proclaiming of the gospel to all" (canon 762).

Of course a valuable teaching technique is the use of video recordings, but the instructor should view the recordings with the preacher, give appropriate comments, and evaluate the criticisms which the preacher has heard in class. My brother, Father Oscar Miller, C.M., offers the following suggestions regarding what to look for when reviewing a recorded homily.

"After reviewing the entire tape recording, the critic should ask whether the overall impression is a good one: Did I get something out of it? Do I feel the presentation brought me a little closer to God? If the answer to these and similar questions is positive, the critic can move on to improvements rather than radical changes. The remarks and questions which follow attempt to enhance the totality of the effect.

"First, what do we see? Does the speaker seem to be at ease? Does his bodily presence create confidence in the congregation? Is he rigid or stiff? Is he too relaxed or sloppy? Shoulders back military style create a stiffness which is an obstacle to good listening. Slumping forward or leaning on the ambo, standing on one foot, shifting repeatedly from one foot to the other, weaving from side to side, repeating insignificant gestures, incipient rather than completed gestures, finger wriggling or waving, looking too constantly or frequently to one part of the congregation — all are distractions. Are the gestures expressive of what is being said?

"In a close-up the critic can look for stiffness around the mouth, taught lines around the eyes, frowning, head held rigidly or constantly moving. Constant eye contact should be maintained during the homily and frequent eye contact during the proclamation of the gospel. Eye contact means engaging the eyes of different members of the congregation and not looking just above their heads. The eyes should convey deep interest in, and care and concern for, the members of the congregation.

"Secondly, what do we hear? Is the speaker too fast or too slow? Is the tone monotonous or over modulated? Is the volume too loud or too soft? Is the style more suited to written composition than to the spoken word? Are pauses meaningful and helpful? Does the speaker "vocalize" the pauses ('well, uh, y'know')? Is the pitch suitable for easy listening? Are the variations in melody appropriate? Is the melody monotonous?

"In order to concentrate on individual aspects of delivery, it is sometimes helpful to turn off the sound and observe the silent picture, and then to turn off the picture and listen to the voice.

"In the final analysis the question is: Did the preacher seem to be in good contact with the people, sharing his thoughts and feelings with them, and eliciting from them a favorable response to his General End and Statement of Aim through an acceptable presentation of his Central Idea?"

"The one who speaks is to deliver God's message" (1 P 4:11).

BIBLIOGRAPHY

*"A little learning is a dangerous thing;
Drink deep, or taste not the Pierian spring."*
Alexander Pope

SELECT BIBLIOGRAPHY

*"This will permit us to concentrate on prayer
and the ministry of the word." (Ac 6:4)*

ATKINSON, O'BRIEN. *How to Make Us Want Your Sermon.* This is possibly the first "view from the pew" type of presentation. The ideas in this kind of book are very helpful.

Bishops' Committee on Priestly Life and Ministry. *Fulfilled in Your Hearing,* United States Catholic Conference, 1982. This brief exposition of the Sunday homily (only forty-seven pages) should be read but it is abstract. Its effectiveness is seriously limited by its failure to support principles by means of examples.

BORDEN, RICHARD C. *Public Speaking As Listeners Like It!,* Harper and Brothers, New York, 1935. Borden helped to free public speaking from the constraints of formal composition. In cryptic phrases he describes the four stages of audience reaction which should guide the public speaker: "Ho hum! Why bring that up? For instance? So what?" If you can find a copy, you will derive profitable enjoyment from this book.

BURKE, JOHN, O.P., editor. *The Sunday Homily,* The Thomist Press, 1966. This book is a compilation of papers delivered at a workshop on "The Renewal in Scriptural and Liturgical Preaching" at Catholic University in 1965.

FINLEY, JAMES F., C.S.P. *Wake Up and Preach!*, Alba House, 1986. Practical advice from one who spent many years preaching missions around the country and on radio and TV.

HARRIS, DANIEL, C.M., and MURPHY, EDWARD, C.M. *Overtaken by the Word*, Rubicon Publishing Co., Denver, 1990. This work is brief, easy to read, very practical, and it was done by two of my Vincentian confreres.

LEE, CHARLOTTE I. *Oral Reading of the Scriptures*, Houghton Mifflin Co., Boston, 1974. An excellent presentation on the oral interpretation of the scriptures.

MACNUTT, SYLVESTER F. *Gauging Sermon Effectiveness*, The Priory Press, Dubuque, 1960. This is a dependable guide which, the author says, "tells you how to improve sermons after you have written them."

MARKQUART, EDWARD F. *Quest for Better Preaching*, Augsburg Publishing House, Minneapolis, 1985. The author is the Pastor of Grace Lutheran Church in Des Moines, Washington. He states that he read 28 books on homiletics which had been recommended by various seminaries. He explains: "Knowing that pastors are busy people and may not have the time to read the most recent literature in homiletics, I have read these books and organized their contents into a teachable whole, bringing their best insights into one compendium on preaching." His explanation reveals the value of his book and I recommend it although, as you might expect, it does not treat of liturgical preaching as understood by the Second Vatican Council.

MONROE, ALAN H. *Principles and Types of Speech*, Scott, Foresman and Co., 1955. Monroe created the "Motivated Sequence," which is a very helpful tool for speech composition. It is, in my view, a sophisticated version of Borden's method.

PHILLIPS, ARTHUR EDWARD. *Effective Speaking*, The Newton Co., Chicago, 1938. This is an old but excellent book. It is very helpful for understanding the principles for achieving unity and coherence and for developing forms of support. If you can find a copy, buy it and read it. I cherish my copy.

SARETT, LEW and FOSTER, WILLIAM. *Basic Principles of Speech*, Houghton Mifflin Co., Boston, 1946. This is an old standard from Northwestern University. It is excellent on both delivery and composition. Make sure you get the 1946 edition. A revision of the work after Lew Sarett's death lessened, rather than enhanced, its effectiveness.

ZINSSER, WILLIAM. *On Writing Well*, "An Informal Guide to Writing Nonfiction," Harper & Row, New York, 1976. This is a practical aid to improving composition, and the principles are readily adaptable to preaching.

Since, as Ecclesiastes notes (12:12): "Of the making of many books there is no end," this bibliography could contain a long list of works on homiletics, some better, some worse, than those mentioned here, but I submit only these few favorites — some new, most old. The old ones are tried and true. Actually I have almost always found it helpful to read any book on homiletics or public speaking. Even though Ecclesiastes also notes that "in much study there is weariness for the flesh," preachers should from time to read books on the theology and practice of preaching. Preaching is so important that I find it worthwhile to have discovered only one helpful idea from an entire book. I trust however, that preachers will discover help, not only in study, but in every form of human experience because there is a homily in everything.